She's an unabashed romantic with a clear-eyed view of love!

She's a woman with a fabulous career who is famous for her skills in the home and the kitchen!

She's a shy person who adores performing for millions!

She's been happy, she's been hurt, but she's never been afraid to love again!

She's a girl from the Tennessee mountains who knows everybody who's anybody in Hollywood!

She's real, she's warm, she's wonderful . . .

Meet Dinah Shore!

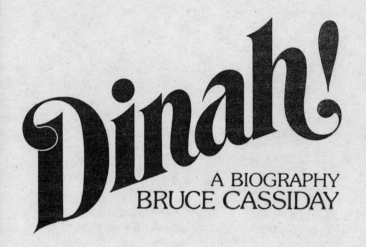

Dinah!

A BIOGRAPHY
BRUCE CASSIDAY

BERKLEY BOOKS, NEW YORK

This Berkley book contains the complete
text of the original hardcover edition.
It has been completely reset in a type face
designed for easy reading, and was printed
from new film.

DINAH!

A Berkley Book / published by arrangement with
Franklin Watts, Inc.

PRINTING HISTORY
Franklin Watts, Inc. edition published 1979
Berkley edition / November 1980

ISBN: 0-425-04675-3

A BERKLEY BOOK ® TM 757,375
Berkley Books are published by Berkley Publishing Corporation,
200 Madison Avenue, New York, New York 10016.
PRINTED IN THE UNITED STATES OF AMERICA

Contents

1

Born on a
Mountaintop
in Tennessee

On a tree-shaded side street in the small Tennessee town
of Winchester, on the western slopes of the Cumberland
plateau, stands a two-bedroom white clapboard cottage.
And it was in a bedroom of that house on March 1,
1917, that Frances Rose Shore was born. Frances Rose,
who later changed her first name legally to Dinah, spent
the first six years of her life there, before the family
moved to Nashville, some eighty-two miles away.

"I have a very fond, distant memory of the living
room of that house in Winchester," the singer recalled.
"You see, that's where my mother taught me the first
reading lessons I had." Her mother used blocks with
ABC's on them and kindergarten primers with big easy-
to-read type.

"Family" meant Frances Rose's older sister

Elizabeth and her father and mother. Solomon A. Shore had been born into a European family of teachers and religious leaders but had left his home to emigrate to America as a young man, settling in Winchester after his marriage to Anna Stein. In Winchester he established a small department store.

The Shores were the only Jewish family in Winchester, and at first they were regarded as ethnic curiosities by the citizens. They had a great pride in their cultural background, and it was their intention to prove that, although they were newcomers to the community, they could be among its best people.

They worked hard at it. Solomon Shore became a leader in the Masons, and Anna in the Eastern Star. By the time Frances Rose was born, the Shores had become integrated into the community, and there was little prejudice against them.

On the surface, the Shores appeared to be an ordinary middle-class white-collar family. But there were disparities that created psychological tensions. Solomon was twelve years older than Anna. Elizabeth was eight years older than Frances Rose. The age differences created an imbalance that decisively affected the relationship of the four.

Besides the age gap, there were personality conflicts. Solomon was a hard-working solid citizen, good at his business. He had succeeded without taking any shortcuts and without the benefit of any lucky breaks. Whatever he earned, he worked hard to get.

Anna was an aspiring opera singer with a marvelous contralto voice. She was also an all-around sports enthusiast. Whereas Solomon wanted security and peace and quiet, Anna wanted "splash." Anna wanted to *be* somebody — exactly who, she didn't quite know.

"Her need for us to impress the world made you wonder if you really were as good as the rest of the world," Frances Rose said.

Solomon Shore was not a demonstrative man. Anna, on the other hand, was spirited, handsome, gregarious, vibrant, and vital. "Name it, and she could do it," remembered Frances Rose. "Horseback riding, tennis, a fine game of bridge, championship golf." When Anna sang, her rich rounded tones shook the room. The girls knew that she studied voice in secret because their father wouldn't put up with singing lessons.

Though he was proud of her accomplishments, he considered them nonessential and frivolous and was furious one day when he found out that Anna had been slipping away to the next town for voice lessons.

"Everyone in this family can sing," he stormed at her. "I don't care about that. But who wastes money taking lessons for such a thing? No one in this family is going to. What are you thinking about, Anna? Going on the stage, maybe?"

Anna was silent.

Different attitudes toward money in husband and wife were also evident: Anna Shore always wanted to spend. Solomon Shore always wanted to save.

The tension between these two strong personalities—the one domineering, serious, hard-working, and without humor, and the other light-hearted, fun-loving, and outgoing—created dissension that was always simmering just below the surface.

And then there was the age and friendship gap between the two daughters. "I know now that my mother had tenderness and love for me, but I wasn't sure as a small child," Frances Rose said. "My sister was eight years older than I was, and from the beginning I thought that she and my mother seemed to have an intimacy that excluded me."

In a home full of such tensions, Frances Rose's life did not start out too happily. And at the age of eighteen months she was suddenly stricken with poliomyelitis. It was many years before the Salk vaccine and other preventatives had been discovered; there was no known cure for the dread disease.

The little girl survived the ravages of the fever, but was afflicted with paralysis in her right leg and foot. Poliomyelitis was treated in those days by what was known as the "Sister Kenny" method, named after Elizabeth Kenny, an Australian nurse who had developed a way of using hot packs and moist applications in conjunction with passive exercise.

"Passive exercise" meant constant massaging of the paralyzed muscles by a therapist. Frances Rose was taken to a therapist who "stretched" the muscles of her leg and foot in an attempt to return them to their proper size and function.

Her mother and father both gave her massages. In addition, Anna taught her daughter how to play tennis and how to swim and sent her to ballet school. This had the effect of acquainting Frances Rose with a life of constant outdoor exercise.

But Anna Shore's emotions were torn between pity and frustration over her ambitions for her child. And on her part, Frances Rose began to feel that her illness had been a disgrace and she developed a sense of shame about it.

"The early experience made me shy and ambitious at the same time," she said. "I would run faster than anyone else, and jump higher. I knew I had to do something to prove myself."

Her efforts to exercise her foot and leg turned her into something of a tomboy. "Rope-skipping was a big pastime for me. I also loved to play ball in the front yard. And I vividly recall riding my tricycle on the sidewalk by the house in Winchester."

The rigid therapy was continued for at least six years after her attack. "I had a mother who wouldn't let me stop. Struggling hard to beat something may have given me a drive I wouldn't have otherwise had."

And the fact that her illness was not ever mentioned

by her family added to her concern over it. "My relatives always kept whispering about me at home, so I never was allowed to forget that something really terrible had happened to me. My inferiority complex stayed with me most of my life."

During those years she took all kinds of exercises. A cousin recalled, "We used to go on family picnics and she would dance barefoot on the sand along the river."

But her recovery was slow and the treatment was painful. "I saw the tears stream down Dinah's face as a very little girl when she thought she would never completely get over the effect of the disease, and that people might notice that she had a limp," her cousin noted.

At one point her father took her to a specialist in New York who worked on her, but the treatment he prescribed was also painful, and the regular exercises and massaging continued.

Dinah kept at it, doing everything she was told, and grimly promised herself that she would conquer this disease—not only conquer it but be as good at sports as her mother was.

"I suppose she'll have to learn to walk all over again," her mother sighed several times in her hearing. With that challenge ringing in her ears, she did learn to walk, to dance, to play tennis, to fence, to swim.

But learning wasn't enough. She always had the feeling that there was something to be ashamed of in her illness, that the other kids wouldn't play with her because she was weaker than they. Winning love and approval became a precept by which she lived every moment of her life.

"The unfortunate thing about me was that I suffered from a desperate desire to be loved, but I was pretty unlovable," she said. "I was constantly singing, dancing, and showing off in a desperate bid for attention and to prove I could do it."

Before she could even talk plainly, she began singing in public. She would climb up onto a counter in her father's little store in front of the customers, and burst into song: "Here I stand with two little chips; who will kiss my pretty lips?"

And she began to understand that not only she, but her family as well, was somehow set apart from the rest of the community. Winchester was a Southern city, predominantly Protestant. It had built-in anti-black, anti-Semitic, and anti-Catholic prejudices.

Frances Rose remembered vividly one night that her father took her out to watch a Ku Klux Klan parade going by on the street. With their hoods on and their spooky sheets, the Klansmen presented an awesome and frightening sight to the young, impressionable girl.

As the sheeted figures marched along, her father leaned over and angrily told her the names of most of the men marching by—many of them friends and neighbors. He knew them from their shoes and the way they walked. Not for nothing was he the owner of a drygoods store that sold all kinds of clothing. It was part of his business to notice the brands of clothes his friends wore.

Frances was surprised at the intensity of her father's rage. He was deeply disturbed and highly incensed. "He never had violent emotions," she said later, "and I couldn't get over his anger that night. I've never forgotten it."

It underlined for her the fact that she was different, too; and "different" people had to strive harder to become "equal." In a way, that understanding impelled her toward achievement. The struggle was not without its toll on her. She grew up chronically underweight, full of bitter frustrations over being on the outside looking in.

When Frances Rose was six years old, her father brought into a large department store concern in Nashville, the capital of the state, and the family packed up and moved there. They settled down in a quiet street in an affluent neighborhood.

By now Frances Rose had started public school.

She still had a limp from the polio attack. Kids, being what they are, made fun of her, not only because of the limp, but because she was a new face in town.

She gritted her teeth and determined to walk correctly without any kind of impediment. It was a self-motivated drive, rooted in the desperate desire not to be "different," and to be accepted, like everyone else.

By the time she was nine years old, she had overcome all difficulties. Her right leg looked almost exactly like her left. Today the only difference visible is a slightly higher arch in the right foot, due to the amount of exercise the afflicted foot was given.

One year later she began swimming nearly every day at Nashville's Cascade Plunge and playing tennis as often as possible to continue strengthening her leg.

Except for her illness, her life as a child was fairly routine. She played the usual games with Bessie, her sister, and she had a cat, a dog, turtles, fish, and birds at various times. But her mother and father did not much care for animals. What Frances Rose really wanted to own was a big dog—the bigger the better—but her father put his foot down.

"It was like he wouldn't let me have a big bike, either," she said. "He was afraid either one would hurt me." She reasoned that he was fearful the poliomyelitis had weakened her to such a degree that she could not properly take care of herself.

During those early years, one thing affected her very much. Both her mother and father, being of opposite temperaments—and short-tempered, high-strung, and highly combative—tended to quarrel constantly. They simply did not believe in keeping any of their thoughts bottled up. Psychologists might have had good words for this ability to bicker without building deep-seated grudges. But Frances Rose did not. The sound of shouting behind closed doors in the house was a nightmare to her. "I always felt I shouldn't express great disagreement or anger. It was impolite."

When she heard them let their anger brim over, she felt pangs of fear. "I was afraid that they were going to separate or something terrible was going to happen—like moving away and seeing all our stability cut from under us."

As a child, she vowed that if she ever married, she would never quarrel, never yell, never make her husband do things he didn't want to do. She determined to become whatever her husband wanted her to be.

When she grew up, her youthful vows were not forgotten. They shaped her life into a pattern that would have astounded and frightened her.

Nashville, in Frances Rose's childhood, was a thriving city, and her father's business ventures went very well indeed. Prosperity was everywhere. It was the Roaring Twenties, a time of enthusiasm, zest, and gaiety in America. The Shores were well off and had a maid and other servants to take care of their needs.

But Frances Rose never had it easy. As she grew into her teens, she underwent a metamorphosis from a bouncy little girl to a skinny, awkward, rather unattractive teenager. "You could really say she was an ugly duckling when she was twelve or thirteen," said a childhood friend. "She was awkward and gawky and not attractive at all. She was skinny, she had a big nose with a hook in it. She had very black hair and a very dark complexion."

In truth, Frances Rose was most sensitive about her looks. "When I was a teenager," she recalled, "all I had to do to realize that I was no beauty was to look in a mirror."

In addition, she hated her name, Frances Rose Shore. In the South, Frances became "Fanny." And "fanny" was a funny word to kids; it meant the human posterior. She suffered for years hearing the kids pun on her name.

"Fanny sat on a tack. Fanny Rose. Fanny Rose sat on a tack. Did Fanny rise? Fanny Rose—Shore!"

It was too much for the young girl. She wanted any other name but Fanny Rose. And eventually she found one. But that was not until several years later, when she had left Nashville and started her career in music.

Music lay in her future. Her inner drive to achieve increased—not only because she was Jewish and had been afflicted with polio, but also because of a competitive instinct she must have inherited from her mother. In time this drive found in music its natural channel.

"I wanted to act, really," she said, "but there weren't any Tennessee Williamses around in those days, and it wasn't easy for a girl with a Southern accent to get work.

"Luckily, I could sing. Every Southern belle learns to sing, just as she learns piano and needlework. It's a wonder I didn't learn to play the harp!"

Instead she picked the ukulele. She took lessons and learned to strum it, singing the popular songs of the day. She took it with her everywhere, even to the public swimming pool, where she serenaded the lifeguards with renditions of "I Can't Give You Anything But Love, Baby."

Anna Shore had a fine contralto voice. Frances Rose imitated her. She sang all the time. In fact, she sang and played when no one really wanted to hear her. In the eighth grade, she got up in the auditorium and sang and played the ukulele in front of the whole school. Her song was titled "My Canary Has Circles Under His Eyes."

Her performance bombed completely. "It was far too sophisticated for my audience," she explained many years later with a rather forced smile. It was no fun to be booed.

"I can't remember when I wasn't singing," she said. "I'd ask my sister Bessie if I could come into the parlor and play the ukulele and sing for her when she had dates." But that triumph too was short-lived. One night she stayed and made a nuisance of herself all during her sister's date. After that she was banished to her room.

She sang for the Ladies' Aid Society to which her mother belonged, belting out "I Can't Give You Anything But Love, Baby." She was received with restrained enthusiasm. Her mother was a long-suffering listener. Anna Shore loved classical music and operatic arias. Frances Rose preferred popular songs, anathema to Anna.

Her father wanted his daughter to be a sociologist, or to train for some other profession. He wanted her to be anything but an entertainer. A performer, in his eyes, was the next worst thing to a bum.

Besides, not everybody thought Frances Rose was a great singer. "Her voice was lousy," a neighbor recalled. "Many people thought she had a terrible voice. 'She'll never get anyplace,' we thought."

When the Shores decided that nothing could stop their daughter from singing, they arranged for her to take voice lessons from a professional teacher. His name was John A. Lewis.

"Mr. Lewis put me into the First Presbyterian Church choir," Frances Rose said, "but that didn't work too well for the rest of the choir, since everything had to be revoiced for me. I'd sung solo so intensively at home that I couldn't get the hang of harmony singing.

"Also, even at that age I was a contralto. I was like a boy who'd become a baritone before his voice changed."

When she was fourteen years old, Frances Rose decided that she was ready for the big time. Church choir singing hadn't worked out as well as she had expected it to. But there were other places to start. In the outskirts of Nashville there was a "real mysterious place," as her friends described it, called The Pines. It was a nightclub that catered to the newly affluent in the city and provided liquor, gambling, and, incidentally, entertainment.

Frances Rose approached the manager and told him that she could sing and would oblige with a number for his patrons if he would pay her ten dollars. She was so determined and so obviously eager to be a singing star that he gave in and told her she could perform.

She didn't tell her parents about it. She knew they would blow the whistle and prevent her from appearing in public.

"I talked a boy friend into swiping his father's car," Frances Rose recalled. "He wasn't too happy about the whole thing, but I had plenty of sweet-talk on hand."

In preparation, she spent over an hour applying makeup to her face, using her sister Bessie's cosmetics, and finally got herself looking fairly good. Then she took her sister's favorite party dress of flowing chiffon and put it on.

It fitted perfectly.

They arrived in the borrowed car at The Pines during a driving rain. Frances Rose ran across the parking lot, her gown trailing in the mud because she didn't have sense enough—or training enough—to hold it up.

Excited and scared, she managed to get out onto the stage. The lights went down and a spotlight focused on her. She felt like fainting. The orchestra started up the introduction to her song, "Under a Blanket of Blue."

"Never will I forget that song," she said later, "because halfway through I looked over at a big party at a corner table, and there, right in the middle, were my father and mother—with their mouths hanging open!"

Instead of fainting, as she thought she might do, she almost died!

The whole song went out of her head, and she just

stood there. Then, magically, the words came back.

Gritting her teeth, she continued, singing her heart out, and finally finsihed heroically. She grabbed the ten dollars she had been promised, and was then delivered into the hands of her parents.

They had been tipped off about her debut, but had decided to let her finish her number before taking her in charge.

"Oh, my!" Frances Rose said. "That was the last nightclub I ever saw for quite a spell!"

The rest of the incident, the lecture part of it, was a big bore to Frances Rose.

"Dear," her mother said. "You're too young to become a torch singer."

Frances said nothing.

"You've got to get your education," her father put in. "I don't mind your singing, but you've got to have something in your head when the music stops."

Frances thought he sounded about like all fathers should sound.

"Please don't think we're being unfair, but we do think you should put more time on your education. Finish high school. Go to college."

She was still excited by the feeling she had had when she stood up to sing in front of all those people. She had been bitten by the bug—it was show business for her from there on in. Yet she reluctantly agreed to obey her parents.

Even at fourteen, she was well on the road to popularity. She had a desperate desire to be accepted, to be praised, to be loved. She had decided that an outgoing personality, a friendly manner, and a determination to excel could make up for her lack of looks and for her Jewishness.

Sports, drama, and singing—she was active in everything that counted in Hume-Fogg High School. She played parts in school productions of *Little Women* and *Outward Bound*. Later she sang a part in a Gilbert and Sullivan operetta. She was even a cheerleader. Everybody went to the football games, and there they could not fail to see Frances Rose as she led them in the yells and shouted encouragement to the players.

"She had such an outgoing, friendly personality that you didn't notice so much how unattractive she was physically," a friend recalled. "Her personality carried her."

She determined to be the all-around high school girl. And it was this determination that brought her to one of the first crossroads of her life. It involved a decision between two important choices. She could opt for popularity, or she could opt for voice training.

Football games were played on Friday afternoons. Frances's voice lessons also came on Friday afternoons. John Lewis could not change his schedule just to suit her. In fact, he said, it was impossible.

Besides, her job of leading the cheers at the football games had always seemed a bit juvenile and barbaric to him. And he didn't like what it was doing to her voice. To his way of thinking, his pupil could either be a singer with a career, or she could be a cheerleader with no career.

He spoke to Frances's mother. "Mrs. Shore, we've come to one of those decisions that has to be made. Either cheering goes out of Frances's life"—here he paused for emphasis—"or I do."

"It's up to Frances," said Anna Shore, knowing that she could only advise and consent, not make the decision for her daughter.

Frances grew up a little at that point. She had always been a stubborn girl: witness her surreptitious actions in debuting at the Nashville nightclub. Her stubbornness made her incensed over what she considered an ultimatum. Why couldn't Mr. Lewis shift the schedule? She thought he was being arbitrary. And that made her angry.

"I've never reacted flabbily to ultimatums," she

told a magazine writer much later. She made the decision promptly.

"Mr. Lewis goes," she told her mother.

By that time her older sister had married Maurice Seligman, a doctor, and had settled in St. Louis to be with him where he was interning at a very good St. Louis hospital. It was a plum of an internship, and he was well on his way to a fine career in medicine.

It was when Frances Rose was about sixteen that the Shore family sustained a blow from which it never fully recovered. Frances Rose was sitting quietly in high school one day when she suddenly experienced a feeling of depression such as she had never felt before. She had what she later described as a "compelling urge to run home." Later, she knew it for what it really was: extrasensory perception, the first of several cases in her life.

"I knew suddenly that my mother was deathly ill."

She told her teacher that she had to leave, but her teacher ordered her back to her seat. Instead Frances Rose disobeyed her and ran down to the principal's office. In tears, she begged to be allowed to telephone her home. The principal agreed, and when the telephone rang, the maid answered.

"I knew immediately from her tone that something was terribly wrong," Dinah recalled. "She said that, yes, Mother was sick. I dropped the phone and ran the whole fifteen blocks home. Mother died just minutes after I got there."

Later the family learned that Anna Shore had been stricken with a heart attack at just about the time her daughter had that feeling of dread in class.

"I believe," she said later, "that as my mother was dying, she was crying out for help and that I heard her because we were so close."

It was an incredible and desperate situation for the surviving members of the family. Solomon Shore was left solely responsible for his young daughter. With a chain of drygoods and notions stores to supervise, not only in Nashville but in nearby towns, he could not be home all the time.

"It's a worrisome and mysterious responsibility for a man to bring up a girl in her middle teens," she said. "Don't forget, I was on the verge of sixteen, the most difficult time for a young girl, a time when resentment is most evident, too."

What happened then made her beholden for life to her sister and brother-in-law. Dr. Maurice Seligman and Bessie moved from St. Louis to Nashville. In doing this, Dr. Seligman gave up his prized post in St. Louis and transferred his internship to the Nashville General Hospital. Bessie took over the supervision and upbringing of her baby sister.

They made a home for Frances Rose. In fact, she said later that her brother-in-law "became more influential in my life than anybody." Although she already had a father, Maurice became a kind of surrogate mother *and* father to her.

The death of Anna Shore settled Frances down a bit. She didn't abandon her musical career exactly, but she let its importance recede into the background. And she took up romance.

"Pisces are always in love," she said. She was a Pisces, of course, being born on March 1. At the age of seventeen, she fell madly in love with the captain of the high school swimming team. The fact that the captain was a student professor who also tutored indigent mathematics students—and Dinah was definitely an indigent in math—helped the budding romance.

"We almost got married," Dinah recalled. "There was a big swimming meet scheduled somewhere in Kentucky, and we were going to run away from it and elope.

"Me and my big mouth. I guess I told too many girl friends about our plans. Anyway, Dad got word. He cut us off at the pass, you might say. Actually, we didn't do bad at the swimming meet, as I remember it. I think I came in second. And I even passed math!''

Even though she was unattractive, she still had plenty of dates in her senior year. A friend who became a minister recalled, "My dates with Frances Rose were always in a crowd . . . she was always the life of the party.''

She graduated as the "best all-around girl" in Hume-Fogg High School.

It was then that Frances Rose took the advice of her father and the Seligmans and enrolled at Vanderbilt University in Nashville, majoring in sociology.

She relaxed a little at college, and went in for sorority and club activities with a kind of euphoria. In fact, her yearbook record at Vanderbilt University upon her graduation in 1938 indicated that she had majored in sociology and was a member and president of Alpha Epsilon Phi Sorority. She was also a member of the Glee Club. And she belonged to the French and German clubs and the Arts Club. She also was president of the Women's Student Government Club. And she became involved in the production of light musical shows for the Masque Club. In addition, she was a member of the sorority fencing team, played basketball, and swam. She was the typical all-American college girl.

Well, not exactly *typical*. She had taken up her music again, and John Lewis was now able to get her to study harder. Her natural contralto voice was maturing, although sometimes in a fit of pique he blamed its hoarse, "used" quality on her excessive yelling during her cheerleading years.

Nevertheless, she was learning how to use her voice more effectively. It was not loud or powerful. It could never fill an opera house. Nor could it fill a concert hall. But it was full and rich and true. Now she began to make it do tricks for her.

She liked to slide up and down the scale in imitation

of Ella Fitzgerald and other black singers. She began to work on a throaty, dramatic style of singing, using it to deliver ballads and blues.

"I used to have a black nursemaid when I was a child," she recalled. "Her name was Yah-Yah. It was Yah-Yah who taught me to swing," she told a newsman years later. "She used to croon to me in a funny way. 'Noodling,' she called it. She even took me to church to hear the congregation sing spirituals."

What finally did come out was a dreamy, rich, slow, thoughtful style of singing. The advantage for her was that each word could mean something to the listener. It was a style eminently suitable to the microphone, which was then just beginning to be used extensively by singers of popular songs.

The microphone was a godsend to Frances Rose, because she still considered herself unattractive—or at least not pretty enough to appear before an audience and wow them with her looks alone. Radio would allow her to sing, put everything into her voice, and not be unnerved at appearing in public before people.

In spite of her enthusiasm for entertaining and her drive to be a star, she did not at that time have much faith in her voice—which was all she really had. "It was just ordinary, and, if you think about it, not really a voice at all."

But that realistic appraisal didn't stop her. If anything, it spurred her on to train her voice more and more.

John Lewis was appearing himself on radio station WSM in Nashville. When Frances was a sophomore in college he induced her to go to the radio station with him. He wanted to show her a typical microphone and explain the science of letting it enhance her voice.

Taking her into an unused studio, Lewis planted her in front of a microphone, told her it was "dead," and accompanied her on the piano while she sang.

It was a set up. The mike was not dead. It was

patched into an audition room in which Beasley Smith, the musical director of WSM, was sitting with several assistants. The audition won Frances a job singing on a five-minute twice-a-week show called "Rhythm and Romance."

It was Beasley Smith who once told her she had an unusual style of phrasing. "I wasn't sure what he meant by that," she recalled thoughtfully.

She hated that name "Fanny," by which she was still known in Nashville. To spite her friends and enemies, she had herself billed as "Fannye Rose Shore," adding the "e" to take the edge off the awful nickname.

"She really had no voice," recalled a friend. "But she had a fantastic personality and tremendous willpower and drive. She was so friendly! If she was driving down the street and saw you driving the other way, she would yell 'Hi' all the way across the street.

"If she saw a friend two blocks away, she would almost have an accident trying to wave and say 'Hello.' "

The radio show was good for her ego. People around Nashville began to know her and to comment favorably on her singing. The theme song of the show was the old standard "Dinah," written by Harry Akst in 1926. Most bands played "Dinah" as a stomp, fast and up-tempo, with the words lost in the shuffle. Fannye, as she was now known, sang the song in a very muted, slow, off-beat way. "I swiped my interpretation from Ethel Waters," she later confessed. But she put a great deal of her own creativity and artistry into the singing of it.

It was during these early days in Nashville that she picked up a learning trick to which she clung all through her singing years. She recorded every song she sang and listened carefully to the playback.

She found that she did not have to strain her vocal chords at all to project a song. It depended on the distance she placed herself from the microphone. And certain qualities of voice came over nicely on the mike. She tried new tricks, listened, and kept the ones she liked. If something offended her, she immediately dropped it, or changed it so that it sounded right.

She was a conscious artist, not particularly an inspired one. She knew exactly what she wanted to do, and when she did it, she used all the help she could get—from her voice teacher, from the microphone, and, later, from her arranger and accompanist. But she never rested. She never said: "This is it. I've made it. This is the way I'll always sing."

The success of her five-minute spots over WSM convinced Fannye that she had talent. She thought that she could become a professional singer. "My ambition was to sing with a band," she said later. But her father most emphatically disagreed.

"There are a hundred singers for every job you're after," he told her. His favorite vocalist of all time was Gracie Fields. Gracie could really belt out a number. He did not think his daughter had that kind of talent. "You'll never hold a note the way Gracie Fields does," he said to her many times.

There was more to it than simply being unable to match Gracie Fields. He was convinced that she not only lacked the vocal equipment to succeed, but also lacked the ability to control the emotional experiences that might come up if she were traveling with a band and singing.

"He thought I was overemotional and therefore vulnerable to designing males," she said. "Looking back, I can see that he knew more about me than I knew about myself."

College took up most of her time in those days. She sang at assemblies, played roles in student musicals, and was busy being one of the popular girls on campus.

In her sophomore year, she fell in love. The object of her affection was the captain of the football team.

The only trouble was, he had plenty of other girls and
didn't particularly want Frances Rose. She took it in her
usual cool, sophisticated fashion—by weeping in public
for days and turning thin and pale from lack of food.
But she finally got over him.

Another boy came along. And this one was different. He was interested in music, and he was interested
in Frances Rose Shore as *herself*, a singer. He helped her
with her songs as much as he could.

One night she had a date to sing a song at an
audition somewhere in Nashville. The song they wanted
her to sing was the tuneful, lovely number, "Stars Fell
on Alabama." The boy agreed to take her to the
audition, and then on to a dance.

In the car she wrote out the words on a piece of
paper to hold in front of her if she forgot them onstage.
"Fannye," he told her, "I don't like to see a singer
referring to notes. I want you to learn the words so you
can sing them from memory."

More to satisfy him than anything else, she
memorized the words as he drove her along to the
station. She knew them letter-perfect by the time they
got there. And she never forgot them.

A year later he left for the Naval Air Corps and
corresponded irregularly with her. It was not until two
years later after Dinah had graduated from Vanderbilt
that she heard from him again. She was in New York at
the time, singing on the radio.

He wrote to tell her he would meet her in New York
for a date, just for old time's sake. His furlough was
due on December 8, 1941, and he would be in town the
second week in December.

He never made it. Two days later Dinah got a wire
from his mother. He had been killed at Pearl Harbor.

"I never sang that song again," she said.

Her voice was improving. In the summer between
her junior and senior years at Vanderbilt, she went up to

New York to attend a convention of her college sorority, Alpha Epsilon Phi. She stayed on for several weeks trying to get a job singing on the radio. She made the rounds of bands, radio stations, and booking agencies trying to sell her talents.

She had a rough time of it. The Depression was still on. Business was improving, but it wasn't really good. There were rumblings of war in Europe. People were unsettled.

She ran from place to place leaving her name and trying to get auditions. Nobody was interested. Again she blamed it on her looks, but she didn't know what to do about them.

Finally her big break came. A producer at NBC wanted to hear her sing. She rushed over to the studio at Rockfeller Center and got all set up to sing. This was the big-time, much bigger than Nashville. This was Gotham City! She was in!

The accompaniment started, she opened her mouth to voice the lyrics, and nothing came out. Absolutely nothing! Her voice was gone. When the accompanist started in again, she was still mute. She had succumbed to the dreaded disease of every singer—mike fright. She had never had it before, but she had it now, at the worst possible moment of her life. She burst into tears and ran out of the studio.

She had blown it—the most important audition of her career. Quite possibly she would never get another chance like that. What had happened? She would never know.

But Fannye Rose never gave up. She was still running around town trying to get another audition when her father got in touch with her. He tried the reasonable approach. "You're going to miss your senior year in college if you stay in New York," he told her.

"I want to be a singer with a band." Fannye reminded him.

"If you'd gotten a job this summer maybe you could work with a band. But you didn't. Come home now and finish school."

She didn't say it, but she knew what her father wanted. He wanted her to settle down and marry some nice local boy in Nashville or go into welfare work when she finished college. Or maybe both.

Keeping her fingers crossed, she tried for several more auditions, but nothing worked out. Discouraged, she took the bus back to Nashville. It was *not* all over, she decided. She would be back and take New York by storm as soon as she graduated.

Her senior year at college was more of the same —dances, shows, parties, and even a bit of studying. She had plenty of dates, too. Being popular was fun. Almost as much fun as singing. But it was not really the same thing.

Although she seemed to settle down at home with her father and her sister and her brother-in-law, a typical 1930's college girl on the surface, in her heart she had determined that she would break away from Nashville as soon as she had carried out her promise to her family.

And that was exactly what she did.

2

New York
on 35 Cents
a Day

Had it not been for her own persistence and the intervention of her sister and brother-in-law, it is quite possible that Fannye Rose Shore never would have left Nashville for the second time to knock on the doors of New York City.

"Daddy didn't want me to break my heart," she said. "Sometimes when you beat your head against a wall your heart takes the punishment."

But Bessie, Maurice, and Frances prevailed against his opposition. Only to an extent, however. He would not advance any money. "You can go," he said, "but you're on your own. When your money runs out, come home and forget singing."

Frances had been dabbling in photography in school, and had purchased a camera and other ex-

pensive equipment. Saddened at having to make
another hard decision between two strong desires, she
sold her camera things, scraped together $253.75, and
bought a one-way ticket to Manhattan.

The Shore family had always been well off, even
for those Depression days, and in Nashville both at high
school or at college Frances had never really had to
count her pennies, much less her dollars. She simply had
not learned the value of money. "There had always
been dollars in my pocketbook," she said, "because
Daddy put them there."

Immediately upon arriving in New York, Frances
did what any decent, respectable daughter of a middle-
class American businessman would do in the Big
City—she got a room at the Barbizon Hotel on
Lexington Avenue.

The Barbizon was then as now a well-run, well-
policed hotel catering to unmarried women working in
New York City. It was expensive in comparison to other
hotels, but its service was excellent, and its security well-
nigh invulnerable.

Frances thought nothing of staying there and
having her meals sent to her room. Needless to say,
her money rapidly ran out.

Meanwhile, she was going from one radio station
to another, one record company to another, one booking agent to another, trying to get some kind of job. It
was the same as it had been the summer before when she
had blown the NBC audition. There were simply no
takers.

"I don't think I ever worked harder in my life,"
she said, "rehearsing and practicing and whipping my
musical style into shape. But at least I had entrée into
audition studios, even though I didn't get anywhere for
months.

"They said I lacked experience. Of course I lacked
experience. I had to get a job to earn experience. For six
months I batted around getting nowhere. I bruised my

knuckles on doors, wore out my fanny sitting around in hard chairs waiting for executives to show up, and often went hungry for lack of funds." She allowed herself 35 cents a day for drugstore sandwiches. They were, by Nashville standards, terrible.

Seeing that her money was disappearing at an undreamed of rate of speed, Frannye Rose bid a sad farewell to the Barbizon and moved to a less expensive hotel. But that turned out to be too expensive too, and she went to cheaper quarters.

Finally she began sharing a one-room apartment with four other career girls who were having about the same kind of luck as she was. "The other girls lived much better than I did," she said, "because they always seemed to have lots of dinner dates. I don't know what was the matter with me, but no one even bought me an English muffin."

At last she got a break. It was actually only a mini-break. It was a chance to sing on one of the New York radio stations—"for no." In other words, to sing for nothing, no recompense.

Although such an arrangement is unheard of today, it was not unheard of in those latter-Depression days. In fact, it was the accepted way in which most young singers got started.

The audition was held at WNEW, an independent New York station—that is, one not affiliated with a network like CBS or NBC. She sang the song she had sung in Nashville, "Dinah." She sang it exactly the same way she had sung it at home, slow and easy, like Ethel Waters, but with a swinging lilt to it.

Listening to her were two station bigwigs, Martin Block, the head disk jockey and MC of "The Make-Believe Ballroom," and Jimmy Rich, the musical director of the station. "Don't call us," they said, "we'll call you."

In fact, they did call. They had forgotten her first name, so they called her the "Dinah" girl, after the name of her audition song. But they got in touch with her and offered her a job singing whenever there was a time slot to be filled. That meant that she would be singing for nothing.

"Experience," she recalled. "There was only one way to get that experience that I didn't have, and that was the hard way. Whenever there was an open spot on the station, I asked for it. I sang under different names, but I sang.

"Those days were the most important in my life, for people thought it was unfair that I worked on the air without pay, but I actually pleaded for the chance." In this way she got the experience she needed, and she got exposure. And at the same time, she got a new name. From the time of her first appearances on WNEW in New York, she called herself Dinah Shore rather than Fannye or Frances Rose Shore.

People who heard her liked what they heard. A radio writer, Herbert Croom-Johnson, became interested in her singing and made a transcription of a song she sang on a WNEW program. He played it for an NBC official, who played it for another, who in turn played it for still another—until all the members of the corporate beehive had heard it.

To her pleasant surprise, she was offered a fifty-dollar-a-week job for a new radio show that was to begin soon, featuring Lennie Hayton's Orchestra. Everything seemed to be coming up roses. Unfortunately, the program failed to materialize. Dinah was out of luck again.

Soon afterward she got a chance to audition for Tommy Dorsey, who had one of the great swing bands of the time. "I hadn't been out of Vanderbilt University very long," she said later, "and I was still wearing bobby socks, a sloppy joe sweater, a skirt, and scuffed saddle shoes when I went to the audition. I don't know how my singing sounded to Tommy, but I know my costume definitely did not go over."

The Dorsey costume fiasco taught her a lesson. She decided that she would change her image for good, become a sophisticate, and wear the right clothes.

"I figured that if they wanted glamour," she said, "I'd give it to them. The New Streamlined Dinah started moving in pretty fast company. I went on dates of all kinds—traveled in a very different circle. I didn't drink or smoke, of course, but went to cocktail parties anyway.

"People kept handing me Manhattans. I kept setting them down here and there, leaving a trail of full glasses everywhere I went.

'One fellow looked at me accusingly. 'You're not drinking,' he said. When he turned his head, I threw the contents of my glass very casually over my shoulder toward a window. It wasn't open. I got the Manhattan all over my dress. It was too much. I ran. Exit the New Sophisticated Dinah. And she never came back. I decided that I'd be myself, even if it wasn't paying off."

Shortly after that, Dinah got another opportunity—this one to audition for Benny Goodman, the "King of Swing" and undisputed leader of the big bands of the era.

The opportunity came from George T. Simon, of *Metronome* Magazine, the musicians' bible. He had heard her sing and had written a piece about her for the magazine. So had the editor of *Down Beat*. She became know as "the darling of *Le Jazz Hot*." It was all very nice, as Dinah said later, but it didn't pay any bills.

On the strength of the stories, one of Goodman's assistants persuaded him to listen to her. Goodman was probably the busiest man in town, doing the Camel cigarette radio show at night and playing regular engagements as well. He was too busy to see Dinah except during his lunch break.

The scene was a bad one. Dinah was trying for the break that might put her over; Goodman was trying to wolf down a lunch so he could get back to the band to work out a difficult arrangement for the show that night. "While I sang for him, he had his mouth full of hot pastrami sandwich," Dinah related. "I understand now how frantic things are when you work in radio and TV, but I didn't know then."

She was undone from the beginning. "Seeing his jaws working on that miserable sandwich with my whole future at stake froze my voice in my throat. I did lousy."

Whatever sank her, she blew the chance to sing with Goodman, just as she had done with Tommy Dorsey. But, worse than the Goodman loss, she suddenly found that she had less than a dollar left in her kitty. Come New Year's Eve there was only one dime left.

Dinah was singing that day at the radio station, and a call came in to the station organist to supply a girl singer for an orchestra playing at an all-night New Year's Eve party. The fee was twenty-five dollars. Did Dinah want it?

Dinah ran out of the station and spent her last dime on a bus instead of going by subway for a nickel. She arrived at her apartment to change her clothes. "I was already singing," she said, "my foot on the first rung of the ladder of success. I had a head full of visions of some great theatrical producer who would see me at the party, take one look and say, 'Just what I want for my new musical!'

She was halfway into her roommate's best dress, which she was borrowing for the occasion, when the phone rang. "The party's off. Sorry, kid," said a voice on the other end.

Dinah sat down on the bed, despondent. She had spent her last cent on the bus ride. She was dead broke. Being broke in Nashville was one thing, but being broke in New York was catastrophic.

She had to call home. The only person around was

the elevator boy. She borrowed a nickel from him, and called her father collect.

"Okay, I quit," she told him. "I'll come home. But I need the fare. I've run out of money."

He was quite reasonable about it. In fact, he would be pleased to send the money, and the sooner he saw his daughter, the better.

Meanwhile, Dinah's sister Bessie wormed her way into the conversation and began arguing with her father. Finally, as Dinah listened in, Bessie persuaded him to send some money to her in New York.

Dinah could hear the argument over the phone. "If you force her to come home now, licked, it will leave an open psychological wound on her soul!" Bessie was saying in her soft but determined voice. Her armchair psychology evidently won over Solomon Shore.

The grumbling patriarch finally agreed to part with fifty dollars to send to Dinah in the city.

Still no luck. Meanwhile, Dinah practiced, keeping her voice in trim, learning new songs that were coming out, and knocking by day on all the familiar inhospitable doors.

Dinah wasn't the only singer performing for free at WNEW. A group of aspiring youngsters were there with her, vying for spots on the sustaining music programs. One fellow singer, who was later to work for years with Jack Benny, was Dennis Day. And another was the young Frankie Laine.

But the one whom Dinah remembered the best was a skinny young kid from Hoboken, New Jersey, named Frank Sinatra. He was pretty pushy, she thought. And he didn't think much of her Southern accent.

The sustaining show Dinah was singing for suddenly got a sponsor, a furniture company that was located in New Jersey. The brass at the factory wanted a New Jersey singer, not a Tennessee mountain canary. They spoke to the station management, and finally

Frank was moved in with Dinah.

"I didn't see the necessity for him at all!" Dinah said later. "It was my show first. And after a few broadcasts, Frank didn't think *I* added much to the program. My accent was all wrong, even for South Jersey—*he* said!"

Frank began to take over. Dinah wouldn't fight. She tended to fade into the background, not wanting to make a big issue of being upstaged. The upshot of the thing was that they both began battling for attention, epsecially when they sang duets together. Both were good, and not everyone noticed the undercurrent of anatgonism. But some listeners did.

One woman wrote, "I enjoy your program very much—all except the love duets. The two kids singing the duets don't seem to like each other. Why don't you get a pair who can do romantic duets together without looking daggers at one another?"

"After that," Dinah said, "we kind of cooled off." But it didn't do much good. The sponsor pulled out and the program changed format. Neither Dinah nor Sinatra was included.

CBS called Dinah back to hear her once again. At the audition she was accompanied on the piano by a professional musician named Martin Freeman, whom everybody called "Ticker." Ticker liked her singing. He told her so.

"The first time I heard her, I thought she was pretty good for blues and ballads," Ticker said later. He seemed to understand instinctively what she was trying to do. He adapted his accompaniment to her singing style. Everybody noticed that she sounded better. So did she.

The CBS brass didn't hire her, but Ticker took her phone number and promised to see her again. He had a couple of arrangements in mind he would like to try out with her, he said, and also several song ideas he would like her to work on.

He was true to his word. Later he joined her and acted as her accompanist and arranger for many, many years.

In January, 1939, five months after she got her sustainer position at WNEW, Dinah struck pay dirt. She was hired to sing in front of Leo Reisman's popular orchestra, which was appearing at the Strand Theater in Brooklyn. The pay was seventy-five dollars a week! She was scared to death, but after she had sung a few notes, she felt like an old pro and continued to the end with increasing confidence.

The only downbeat thing that happened during that first engagement was that almost as soon as she had the seventy-five dollars in her pocket, a pickpocket took sixty dollars of it, and she had to borrow money to get through the week.

But she had now done what she had set out to do when she first came to New York. She had gotten a job singing with a name band. In fact, when the lights went up after she had finished her first number, she saw her father in the front row of the theater in the audience, clapping like mad for her. That made her feel like a million dollars.

She even got her first *Variety* notice. It was mixed, as was usual. "After a short band number," the review said, "the gal vocalist, Dinah Shore, is on for a single song, 'Won't You Hurry Home.' Nicely gowned, sells a song passably, and has an unaffected ease of manner, but doesn't pile up much of a wallop for the windup."

Shortly after her appearance with Reisman, Dinah was contacted by Xavier Cugat's manager. Cugat had a Cuban band that specialized in "south of the border" music, but also did regular pop tunes. Cugat wanted her to make a record of one of his new songs.

"I paid her twenty dollars a record," Cugat recalled. "The very first record Dinah Shore ever made was with the Cugat Orchestra!"

There are two versions of the rest of the story. One

identifies the song as "The Breeze and I," and the other
as "Thrill of a New Romance." You can believe
whichever version you want to. In fact, the two songs
may have been flip sides of the same record.

Dinah was so nervous when she had finished her
first record, and there was so much racket around her
with the maracas clacking and the castanets going, that
she couldn't hear what the sound engineer was asking
her. "Is your name Dinah Shaw?" was what he really
asked.

"That's right," she replied, thinking he was trying
to say "Shore" in his thick Brooklyn accent. And that
was the way the labels came out: "Vocal by Dinah
Shaw."

"It was a good thing I didn't make my first record
with Artie Shaw," Dinah mused. "That would
probably have come out: 'Artie Shore's Orchestra;
vocal by Dinah Shaw.' Now *that* would have been a
collector's item!"

Things started happening very fast now. Ben Bernie
called her for an audition. Bernie's orchestra was one of
the top bands of the time. Called the "Old Maestro," he
he had been on radio for what seemed like centuries. His
easy style of announcing, and his humorous "voice-
overs" during the introductions to the numbers, had
won him a place in the big band firmament.

When Dinah sang for him, Bernie liked her style
and hired her to sing with his orchestra on his CBS network show. It was called "The Half and Half Tobacco
Hour," and it was sponsored by the American Tobacco
Company. Ironically, Dinah didn't smoke, but who
could *see* a radio star anyway?

Her debut took place in March, 1939. It was almost
back to back with her swan song, two weeks later!
American Tobacco was run by a fantastic character
called George Washington Hill. Hill was satirized unmercifully but accurately by Frederic Wakeman, in a

novel called *The Hucksters*. He was president of the company and thought he knew far more about talent than the people he had hired at great expense to judge it for him.

He listened religiously to the shows his company sponsored, and he grumbled and growled at his radio set, and at his wife (who always listened with him) whenever anything struck him badly. The violins were too loud. The horns were flat. The announcer's voice had a burr in it. As he listened, he took meticulous notes.

When Dinah came on, Hill almost went through the ceiling. The "girl vocalist" was singing too slowly. The "girl vocalist" was singing too softly. The "girl vocalist" had a funny accent. The song she was singing was "Leaning on the Old Top Rail," by Nick Kenney, which was not exactly a stomp tune. But Hill owned the company, so he was the arbiter of all musical taste. "Get her off of there!" he cried to his agency.

To Ben Bernie's credit, he tried to fight the ouster of his singer because he believed in her, but Hill put on the pressure and reminded him who was the boss signing the paychecks. Eventually the "Old Maestro" caved in and let her go.

There's a sequel to the story. Some years later, after Dinah had proved herself to better judges than Hill—namely, the American public—she was hired once again to sing as a guest star on a Hill program, this one the famed "Your Hit Parade."

"I went on the first night, my knees shaking," Dinah related. "I thought sure he'd remember me and scream, 'Get her off of there!' again. But he didn't." What was more, Dinah demanded and got $2,500 for the stint on "Your Hit Parade." Her salary at NBC at the time was $150 a week.

Back in 1939 there were some lean months ahead for Dinah, but in the summer she signed a contract as a recording artist for RCA Victor. Then in August NBC hired her for one of its network radio programs, on a sustaining basis.

She cut a couple of sides for Victor on the Bluebird label, and she sang on the NBC program. And *Variety* was nicer to her than it had been when she appeared with the Reisman band.

"[Dinah Shore] ranks with the best vocalists broadcasting has to offer," the writer said. "Voice is imbued with warmth and flexibility which is coupled to an appealing, distinctive style and good arrangements. Enunciation also rates, it being clear even in the speediest tempos."

The records sold reasonably well, according to RCA. Dinah didn't think the sales figures were exceptional at all. "Daddy bought them," she said. "For a long time I don't think anyone else did."

Shortly after the sustainer started, Dinah was approached to sing with what the press agents of the time called an "all-electric orchestra." It was the precursor to what we now know as the "amplified" rock band. The trick of converting vibrations of strings and reeds and horns into electric pulsations and then amplifying them was a new thing then. It took quite a while to catch on—really, except for Alvino Rey and his electric steel guitar, up to the time of the Beatles in the 1960's.

Newspaper stories on Tom Adrian Cracraft's All-Electric Orchestra described the process: "The original vibrations are picked up electrostatically, translated into electrical voltages, and then into sound by amplifier, controls, and reproducer."

The all-electric band was a novelty at the 1939 New York World's Fair. "The conductor, instead of waving a baton at the musician, plugs it in at a switchboard and calls the trombone when he wants it to take a solo!" the newswriter recorded in stunned disbelief.

Caesar Petrillo's musician's union had fits. Its officials feared "robots" would take over musician's jobs—forgetting that each electrically amplified instrument had to have a musician operating it. And "real" musicians were horrified.

Not so Dinah. In September she made a debut with the "wall-plug outfit," as a *Daily News* writer termed it, and sang through several radio shows on NBC with the organization.

A New York *Daily News* critic who caught her on the show liked her, too. "Dinah's voice," he wrote, "is smooth as silk and shows off today's tunes to their best advantage."

About this time Dinah got a job singing with Peter Dean's jump band at Nick's in Greenwich Village. George T. Simon, still trying to get Dinah a niche, played her up to Woody Herman, who had started to build up a reputation with his band after a shaky start and needed a vocalist.

Herman went down to Nick's with Simon and listened to Dinah sing for Dean. It didn't take.

"I thought she'd be great," Simon recalled. "But Woody, after hearing her, felt differently. We still kid about it. Why? Because he missed hiring Dinah Shore." And that was something to miss!

Dinah was rehearsing in a music publisher's office one afternoon, and one of her admirers suggested that it was about time she signed up with a radio-talent agent to handle her career. He even gave her a recommendation to take along with her.

"I went to that agent's office to audition," she said. The agent listened, and liked what he heard. But there was a drawback: her voice was the only thing he liked about her.

"I'll only consent to handle you if you get rid of that corny name, Dinah," he said.

By now Dinah had become quite attached to her adopted name. It certainly beat Frances, Fanny, or even Fannye. And the big man's tone struck a resonant chord of warning in Dinah's psyche. It sounded exactly like the ultimatum her music teacher had given her during her high school days. "I kept my new name," she reported.

By now Ticker Freeman had become Dinah's permanent accompanist and arranger. He went along with her to every audition. In fact, he set up a few of them himself. He went over each song with her line by line. And he taught her vocal and stylistic tricks she had never known existed. More important even than being her accompanist and arranger, he became her confidante, an alter ego to boost her up when she was down.

"If I failed an audition—and, boy, did I fail them!—I could tell Ticker," Dinah said. "I could cry my eyes out. He wouldn't think any the less of me. He gave confidence to go ahead and sing *my* way—be myself. Now I don't know where his style stops and mine begins."

It was a style that was catching on. And Dinah Shore's time had just about arrived. In February, 1940, the NBC Blue network started a music show that was destined to become an overnight sensation among a small but dedicated group of blues and jazz fans.

The Blue network was NBC radio's "second" network. The original network was called the "Red." The Blue was eventually disallowed by the Federal Communications Commission on the grounds that NBC was creating a monopoly by having two separate competing organizations owned by the same management. The NBC Blue was separated from the company and became the ABC radio network.

The music show NBC started in 1940 was called "The Chamber Music Society of Lower Basin Street." It was actually a spoof on the Deems Taylor scholastic approach to music. Milton Cross, who was the commentator for the Metropolitan Opera Company on their Saturday broadcasts, eventually became the commentator of the Lower Basin Street show. Deems Taylor's "three B's" were Bach, Brahms, and Beethoven. Basin Street's "three B's," upon which the "Society" was based, were "barrelhouse, boogie-woogie, and the blues."

Jokes abounded in the commentary. Not only were the clichés of musicianship and oratorio lampooned with irrepressible glee, but bad puns and gags came a mile a minute between songs. For example, the commentator would break into a chat about a new boogie-woogie number with, "A Bostonian looks like he's smelling for something; a New Yorker looks like he's found it."

After the horseplay, in which he would subject the phrasing, tune, harmony, and general structure of a popular blues song to the most minute musicological analysis, the commentator would introduce the artist who would perform the tune.

Dinah Shore was known from the start as "Mademoiselle Dinah Diva Shore." She was billed on the first show as a performer "who starts a fire by rubbing two notes together." The musical directors were Paul Lavalle and Charles "Corn Horn" Marlowe. Later on Henry "Hot Lips" Levine became conductor. The fun and spice of the program notes that Milton Cross read later in the life of the program were the work of Welbourn Kelly.

"Kelly's program notes were the best part of the show," Dinah said. "His takeoff on the Deems Taylor-type of running musical commentary was sheer genius. When I did the show, that commentary was delivered by a boy named Gene Hamilton. After I had left, Milton Cross took over."

One memorable meeting took place. The program played W. C. Handy's blues tunes one night, and the famous jazz composer was to be on hand. Dinah sang "Memphis Blues"—one of her favorites—and at the end of the program, Handy came up to her, tears in his eyes, and said, "My dear, 'Memphis Blues' was never

really sung before. You've turned the clock back thirty
years for me.''

Dinah was on the show for only two months, but
during that time she became a nationally known radio
star. Critics were enthralled by the "limpid tones and
halting rhythms, colored now and again by husky
timbre and delivered with dramatic poignancy." She
had made a number of phonograph records, too, and
she was beginning to make money.

The reason she left the Lower Basin Street show
was that her biggest break to date suddenly came along:
a contract on the Eddie Cantor show. With it, ironically
enough, came two of three other breaks that ordinarily
would have made any performer euphoric: guest appearances on the "Shaefer Revue" and on Raymond
Paige's "Musical Americana."

"Not since the time I was graduated from Vanderbilt and received three proposals of marriage within
two days have I had so exciting a week as the second in
September, 1940," Dinah told *Time* magazine. There
were no details about the three proposals, but it made
good copy. "So many things happened, I was positively
dizzy.

"For one thing, I opened at the Paramount Theater
and saw my name up in lights—on Broadway, mind
you. Then I was signed to a long-term contract. My contract for the Eddie Cantor program came through. And
I was signed to make two guest appearances—one on
the 'Shaefer Revue' and the other on Raymond Paige's
"Musical Americans.' All in one week!"

It was the Eddie Cantor show that boosted her into
lasting fame.

3

Yes,
My Darling
ASCAP

By 1940 Eddie Cantor had become one of the estalished names in network radio, if not *the* established name for the introduction of new talent.

Cantor came up through vaudeville and burlesque, where he sang, danced, and told jokes. For years he performed in blackface with Gus Edwards, and then continued on as a star in Flo Ziegfeld's *Broadway Follies*. In 1926 he made the first of his many motion pictures. He was the first star of vaudeville and burlesque to make it big in radio. Appearing as a guest star on Rudy Vallee's "Fleishmann Hour" on February 5, 1931, he was instantly recognized as a natural for the new medium by radio executives.

On September 13, 1931, Cantor bowed in "The Chase & Sanborn Hour" on the National Broadcasting Company. The show continued in the Sunday night slot three years. Rubinoff and his orchestra backed up Cantor and his guest stars each week.

After the show went off the air, Cantor reappeared, first in the half-hour "Pebeco Toothpaste" each Sunday in 1935; then on the "Texaco Oil Show" in 1936; and, in 1937, on the "Camel Cigarette Show" on Wednesdays.

During the runs of his various shows, Cantor introduced unknown singing stars, including Deanna Durbin and others. Regular comics on the Cantor shows were Bert Gordon as "The Mad Russian" and Harry Einstein as "Parkyakarkas." In 1939, Cantor was suddenly thrown off the air for certain remarks he had made at the New York World's Fair about some government officials. (The feisty little comedian had called them "Fascists.") But in 1940, NBC hired him again for Sal Hepatica. The show was called "Time to Smile."

It was to this show that Dinah Shore was signed as the regular singing star in April, 1940, when it debuted in its weekly series. Dinah was ecstatic at continuing on national radio in a more popular slot with a well-known radio and movie star. True to form, she immediately plunged in and worked in painstaking fashion to succeed in the new show.

"You wouldn't believe it," Cantor said. "I never knew anybody who worked so hard. Every week she showed up with twenty new songs. She'd rehearsed them, she'd learned them, and she wanted to sing all twenty to me, so I could pick out *one* for the show!"

Dinah herself was aware of the amount of time she spent on perfecting her art. "I suppose you can't blame people for the impression they have," she wrote. "They hear me sing a tune on the Eddie Cantor program, and it runs perhaps a minute and a half. Then they figure that I get a nice fat salary for that ninety seconds of singing.

"What they don't think about is all the work and preparation that goes into that single performance.

"First there's the matter of selection of the song. No singer picks up the first tune that comes to hand and says, 'Well, I'll sing this on the program.'

"A singer's popularity depends on her ability to make listeners happy by giving them what they want. That means I've got to know what listeners want and I do that by studying fan mail and reviews.

"Secondly, there is the matter of performance. Learning the song is only part of it, yet this entails hours and hours of constant practice. There comes first rehearsal with the orchestra and a second rehearsal and finally a dress rehearsal.

"Sometimes the 'paper' arrangement doesn't work out in performance and that means revision.

"All in all, I should think I put about twenty solid hours of work into a song that takes me perhaps ninety seconds to sing!"

Dinah wasn't kidding when she wrote the foregoing comments, which appeared in *The Baton*, because she put in her time working as hard as anybody in the business. And, in between appearances on the show, she signed on for nightclub performances, just to keep improving. She liked to study immediate audience reaction to new songs and new vocal tricks she was trying out.

Besides that, Cantor wasn't just any employer. He took a personal interest in Dinah, teaching her some very valuable basic show business lessons. Dinah had always pushed herself and tried terribly hard to do everything the best way she could. Her singing had a bit of the same eager-beaver quality she developed when she decided to be the best all-around girl at Hume-Fogg High School.

Unfortunately, pushing always came through to an audience. People would become unnerved when an entertainer was perspiring and trying to make them applaud. Cantor warned Dinah that she was trying too hard and that she came over pushy. He made her relax, slow down, take it easy.

"Dinah, with a voice like yours, you don't need to be jealous of anyone. Have you ever heard of a man hitting the tape first in a 440-yard race and looking back to see what the *other* runners are doing?''

She got the point. She had been working with studio orchestras and with bands playing background to her records, but she had never really learned how to sing in a relaxed fashion to a large audience, and really *entertain* them so they enjoyed it.

"The trick is," Cantor explained, "to try to make them think you're *enjoying* what you're doing. Then they, in turn, become swept up in your enjoyment, and enjoy your fun vicariously."

As she learned to loosen up, she learned to be amused at herself, too. That was no mean trick for Dinah. She had never been amused at herself before. She had taken herself very seriously. She had taken her popularity very seriously. She had worked hard and done everything she could to make people like her.

It was a reversal for her. And the trick worked.

"I have found that if you give everything you've got, honestly, just for the pleasure of giving, everything else takes care of itself," she said.

She also was learning some other show business tricks—for example, how to read dialogue. Most of the radio shows of the time used lead-ins for songs. In between the musical numbers, the guest stars and the singers on the program were required to participate in "skits" that tied the program together.

In that era most of the dialogue was pretty corny, relying heavily on "puns," or plays on words. The reason for that was simple. Radio appealed only to the ears. A sight gag meant nothing. But a play on words could be understood by the millions listening in. And the puns had to be broad and obvious to be understood.

One of Dinah's skits with Cantor went as follows:

DINAH: "Mr. Cantor, I'm having a lot of trouble milking this cow."
CANTOR: "Dinah, if you want to milk the cow, all you need is a little jerk."
DINAH: "Oh, are *you* going to help?"

CANTOR: "Just step aside and watch an expert!"
DINAH: "Do you know how?"
CANTOR: "Do I know how? Dinah, you are now
            gazing at the Gene Krupa of the
            milking set. When a cow sees me, she
            just rolls over and moos, 'Beat Me
            Daddy, Eight to the Quart!' "

Dinah learned how to stress the proper words, how
to make the jokes obvious, and how to work with the
pros. The reference, incidentally, in Cantor's last line,
was a play on the title of a popular musical number of
the time; "Beat Me Daddy, Eight to the Bar," a great
boogie-woogie number played by Freddie Slack. And
Gene Krupa was Benny Goodman's drummer, who later
went out on his own. It all goes to show how evanescent
and perishable the dialogue of the era was.

Shortly after the show started, Dinah, under Cantor's tutelage, sang a song Jack Lawrence had adapted
from an old Russian folk song. Lawrence's American
version was titled "Yes, My Darling Daughter."

When Dinah introduced the song on the Cantor
show, she was also asked to make a record of it for RCA
Victor on the Bluebird label. She sang the number on
the air just a few days before ASCAP, the music com-
posers' trade union, boycotted the radio networks in a
historical move to prevent the playing of any ASCAP
tunes before coming to an important and highly controversial agreement on rates and rights of songs.

"Yes, My Darling Daughter" was one of the best
of the new tunes to come out. A ton of letters came in to
the studio asking Dinah to sing it again on the air. But it
was an ASCAP song, and *nobody* could sing it.

However, Dinah's Bluebird *record* was not under
restriction, even though it could not be played on the
air. Suddenly the record began selling like mad in the
record shops. Eventually it sold about half a million
copies. At that time, any sale in those figures was a
phenomenon.

It was her first hit record, and it became a hit through a series of weird flukes that she called "Dinah's luck." Because of it, she was well on her way to the biggest record sale of her career to date.

"Its success made me relax a little," Dinah recalled. "Not inside, but outside. I stopped trying to be so frantic up front. I found out it was more important to sing to a lot of people and make them feel good than to get the same feeling myself."

She made dozens of other records, particularly of songs she sang on the Cantor show. It was a time when every corner malt shop and diner in America had a juke box in it.

By the fall of 1940, Dinah's voice was known to millions of Americans through the juke boxes, through Cantor's radio program, through disc jockeys on radio shows, and through home phonographs playing her records.

Success was assured to her now. Her sister and brother-in-law moved up to New York to be with her. The three of them lived in an apartment in Forest Hills, Long Island. The only outward sign of affluence was a zippy maroon Packard roadster that Dinah bought with her first bonus money from the Cantor radio show.

In the past if her voice failed as it had during her first NBC audition, she died inside, burst into tears, and ran out of the studio without saying a word. Now she learned to kid herself a little. At one of her performances in a nightclub, she suddenly developed a hoarse throat.

The song started, she tried to sing, but she couldn't utter a word. She waved the orchestra off, and took the mike in her hand. "Folks," she said with a smile. "Have you ever had a frog in your throat? Well, I've got the great grandaddy of all frogs in my throat right now. He'll go away in a moment. But you'll have to be patient with him. Okay?"

Everybody laughed. They were with her.

In a moment she started the orchestra again, and

she sang the song she had tried before. She brought down the house. Not every entertainer could stand off to one side and observe the way she had learned to.

It was a trick that would stand her in good stead through the many years ahead.

Through the Cantor show, other songs came along. In 1940, Johnny Mercer wrote the words to a great tune by Harold Arlen called "Blues in the Night," the theme song for a Warner Brothers movie released as *Hot Nocturne* but later, and successfully, re-released as *Blues in the Night*. When Dinah sang it on the Eddie Cantor show, the response was fantastic. Her record of it once again broke sales figures, although it did not sell quite as many as "Yes, My Darling Daughter" had.

In that same year, there was a special Dinah Shore Day at the New York World's Fair. In 1941, *Motion Picture Daily* conducted a poll to find the country's best girl vocalist. Dinah Shore won, hands down.

After her success on the Cantor show, the NBC Blue network signed her to her own fifteen-minute Sunday songfest; that show ran through 1942.

Many things were happening to the country in 1942. The bombing of Pearl Harbor occurred on December 7, 1941, and shortly after that the United States declared war on Japan. Japan's axis partners, Germany and Italy, immediately declared war on the United States, which "reluctantly" retaliated.

The entertainment business immediately geared itself to serve the rapidly burgeoning armed services in the United States and to entertain the troops sent overseas to fight. It was only natural that Dinah's rising popularity should make her one of the favorites of the troops.

By now her style had solidified somewhat. Cantor's tutelage was asserting itself. One critic said, "When she sings, she sounds as though she means every word—and means every word for you, personally." "What Dinah's voice has that other voices haven't," *Time* wrote, "is an incendiary quality that somehow gives each listener the illusion that she is singing to him alone. This quality—once described as 'starting a fire by rubbing two notes together'—is no acquired trick, but an act of musical intimacy.''

She explained her throaty singing style herself by saying that blues were "fundamental, instinctive." "I'm a pop singer," she told Pete Martin later in a magazine interview, "but there are different kinds of pop singers. There are beat pop singers and there are lyric pop singers. A lyric pop singer is one who tells a story with feeling when he sings. He thinks about and cares about the words. I interpret both ways: lyric pop and beat." Basically, she admitted, she was a "blues singer."

Networks were stealing stars from each other even in those early days of broadcasting. In March 1941, the producers of the Charlie McCarthy radio program, the "Chase & Sanborn Comedy Hour," wanted to sign Dinah as a singer on the show. The new show would pay her $750 a week. Cantor was paying her less than that, enough less that it was probable he would never make up the difference, no matter what.

Cantor had apparently forgotten to take up her option in writing. Dinah had a half-dozen advisors and managers, all of whom wanted to go in different directions to get to the objective: big money. Dinah was caught in the middle. The squabble that resulted settled absolutely nothing.

During the hassle, Dinah caught a cold and was laid up in bed with laryngitis. She was in the hospital when the matter was taken to the American Arbitration Association. The AAA decided that Cantor had taken up the option, even though he had not put it down in writing. That meant that Dinah was out the difference between $750 a week and what Cantor was paying her.

When he heard the decision, Cantor sent her flowers at the hospital. To sweeten the smell of the flowers, he told her he was raising her salary. Dinah wired him back: "You're a darling. I hope all my bosses are as 'bad' as you are."

Dinah made a nostalgic visit to her old home town of Nashville in March, 1942. A war bond rally was being held, and they needed a star. She was selected unanimously. Local dignitaries met her at the railroad station. Her father was as excited as she was. Crowds cheered everywhere. She walked down a big red carpet from the train to one of the biggest limousines in town. A procession of local bigshots began driving through town. A motorcycle corps escorted the procession into Church Street, which was Nashville's Fifth Avenue.

At the scene of the rally, Dinah was all ready to entertain. The accompaniment started, she stepped up to the microphone—and burst into tears. She couldn't sing a note. She thanked everybody and shed more happy tears as they cheered their mute star.

By the fall of 1942, Dinah had become the number one female blues singer in the country. She was queen of the juke boxes, "within an inch of Bing Crosby," as *Time* said. She was chosen Queen of the Brooklyn Dodgers, Queen of Manhattan's famed Seventh Regiment, and was Sweetheart of more army camps than she could remember. At the Manhattan Butlers and Maids Ball she was named "The Girl We Wish Would Come To Dinner."

In 1942 a group of magazine writers estimated that Dinah Shore was making about $115,000 a year—an enormous sum in those days. Her business affairs were being handled by what these writers called "a board of five."

In point of fact, Dinah's financial affairs were in very bad shape. Not being particularly astute in managing money, she was drifting along and letting incompetent people manage her finances.

It was her brother-in-law who first heard of the trouble and who knew that it would probably get worse. Dr. Seligman finally decided he needed professional help with Dinah's increasing income. Almost everyone Dinah had come in contact with—her hairdresser, network executives for whom she worked, her arranger, her booker—had managed to convince her that he or she should have a slice of her income in return for their services. She was cut up in so many ways she resembled a wedding cake.

One of the best lawyers Dr. Seligman knew as Henry Jaffe, an attorney for the American Federation of Radio Artists. Jaffe took a look at the books, paled visibly, and began toting up figures on big sheets of paper. Later he said that Dinah had got herself carved up into so many pieces that she only owned ten percent of herself!

The attorney waded in and managed to extricate her from the impenetrable legal thicket into which she had been lured. From that moment on, Jaffe became her attorney, her business manager, and later on her producer.

It was late in 1942 that the inevitable happened. Dinah Shore was known in every home in the land. Her records were selling in the thousands. Her voice was heard everywhere. Hollywood producers began to take notice. With some nudging from Eddie Cantor, no mean box office draw himself, Warner Brothers decided to take a closer look at Dinah. The executives at Warner Brothers liked what they heard, and enough of what they saw, to deal. They wanted her to appear in a new Eddie Cantor picture.

Dinah's contract with Warner Brothers was a good one. Even the rough-and-tough Jaffe approved. So did the Seligmans. It was good enough to enable Dinah and her sister and brother-in-law to pull up stakes and move permanently to the West Coast.

Many of the radio shows at the time originated from Los Angeles. This enable actors to work in both radio and the movies. The Cantor show moved from New York to Los Angeles.

The Seligmans took a house in Beverly Hills, and

helped Dinah get set up in Hollywood. She selected a duplex, where she moved in with several other radio actresses and singers.

In the flat with her lived Shirley Mitchell, who played a Southern widow on "The Great Gildersleeve." Kitty Kallen, a singer with Jimmy Dorsey's orchestra, lived there part of the time. Shirley Mitchell, who sang on the "Rudy Vallee Show," was also a paid-up tenant. Marian Crain, nicknamed "Rufus," lived with Dinah; she came from the South too, and became Dinah's personal secretary and confidante.

The personnel of the apartment changed from time to time, with actresses and singers coming and going, as did the visitors.

Orson Welles lived next door for awhile, and would drop in now and then—especially when he heard Dinah singing and trying out new numbers. Residents and visitors had a special name for the digs; they called it "The Charm School." It was known by that name for as long as Dinah lived there.

It was pretty much a Grand Central Station in miniature. Two or three evenings a week the place was jumping with song writers, pluggers, arrangers, musicians, actors, and lonely servicemen whom the girls had invited in for the evening.

A great deal of activity was going on out in Los Angeles to provide entertainment for the servicemen stationed in and around the Southwest. The countryside was dotted with marine bases, naval bases, and infantry and air corps training commands.

In fact, the whole country was on a wartime footing by October, 1942. In New York the famous Stage Door Canteen had opened up, with Broadway stars helping out in person to serve GI's of all kinds. In Hollywood, the Hollywood Canteen opened up in November, with actors and actresses from the film studios serving food, washing dishes, and dancing with servicemen.

Dinah Shore, along with hundreds of other en-

tertainers, was scheduled to appear at the opening of the
Hollywood Canteen. It was a busy time for her. A week
before that, she actually sang at seven different shows
for soldiers in and around Los Angeles.

She loved the work, because she got to meet so
many people—especially soldiers and sailors. In spite of
the money she was making and the popularity she had
achieved, she had not really changed all that much from
the hometown girl from Nashville.

Visiting GI's had established a popular hangout
near the Vine Street Brown Derby where they would
watch the girls walk by going up to Hollywood
Boulevard or down to Sunset. Dinah loved to come
through there. She would reach right out and greet shy
soldiers with her "magnolia" accent; "Hi, ya, soldier.
My name's Dinah. What's yours?"

One story said that she was traveling through the
Mojave Desert on the way to an appearance at an army
camp far out in the boondocks when she passed a one-
man sentry box in the desert. She ordered the car
stopped, and got out to talk to the soldier who manned
it. Then she sang a group of numbers for him.

Now, suddenly, Dinah was in love again. It happened the way it always seemed to happen in those days
of hectic activity when the country was pounding its
plowshares into swords. She met a certain GI and
decided he was the one for her.

Ticker Freeman didn't like his looks. He told her
so. "He's a phoney," said Ticker. "Don't let him make
a fool of you."

Dinah blazed right up, unusual for her, and evi-
dence of the deep feeling she had for the new man.
"Don't you talk like that to me! This one's *different*."

"He'll break your heart," Ticker warned.

Dinah was so angry she stomped out of the studio.
She refused to speak to Ticker for several weeks. She
got another accompanist and arranger.

Then the blow fell. The GI suddenly disappeared,
not even telling Dinah he was leaving. She had no idea

where he had gone until a letter came from his home town. He was there, and he was married to his old hometown sweetheart!

Dinah cried her eyes out. It was a bitter pill to swallow. The worst of it was that she had to crawl back to Ticker and apologize. "Ticker, I promise to listen to you in the future," she told him.

And she did. That was the last time she had a serious argument with Ticker Freeman. It was also the last flaming love affair she had before the really big one in her life.

In spite of her heartbreak over the serviceman who had run out on her, Dinah spent most of her life now entertaining troops. The activity was hectic, but she found it extremely rewarding.

She appeared in person at camps, at hospitals and at all kinds of service centers. And she sang on the radio for the GI's, too.

A young man named Glen Wheaton, assigned to the War Department, conceived a show for the Armed Forces called "Command Performance." It was his idea to beam radio shows to the armed services all over the world by shortwave transmission. The War Department gave him the go-ahead in 1942, and footed the bill. The cost of the weekly show came to $75,000 a week, no small potatoes in those days.

All the talent was donated. Stars of CBS and NBC cooperated, each network supplying the talent as it was asked for. The gimmick of the show was an excellent one. Any GI anywhere could write in and request a song, a skit, a joke, anything he wanted from any star he desired.

For example, one wrote in and wanted to hear actress Carole Landis sigh. She sighed for him. Another wanted to hear the sounds of Fifth Avenue at noon. The show obliged. Another wanted to hear a slot machine—a one-armed bandit—cough up a jackpot. He got it. And naturally, plenty of them wanted to hear their favorites singing songs.

During the first year the show was on, Dinah Shore made more appearances than any other performer.

This was the point in her life at which Dinah Shore suddenly changed. Her physical appearance actually underwent a metamorphosis. It was the studio brass that orchestrated the change, with the help of the Warner Brothers makeup department.

The camera lens had found a number of the flaws in Dinah's face. She was a healthy young woman, and her body photographed beautifully. Her voice was already a prized commodity, recorded flawlessly, and certainly needed no change.

Her face was another story. A study of her screen test showed that her face needed a number of improvements if it were to photograph well.

Item: Her jet-black hair was all wrong. She wore it in a high pompadour. "Something I borrowed from Ginger Rogers, I think," Dinah said. "They were called cow-flop hairdos then." The pompadour was built up with rats and falls to make it high enough.

Item: Her complexion was naturally quite dark, almost swarthy. The combination with her jet black hair made her photograph much too dark.

Item: Her brown eyes were not made up correctly to accentuate their attractiveness. Her eyebrows were too heavy and flat for the shape of her face.

Item: Her nose was too long and it had a quite noticeable hook in it. It photographed badly from the sides and made her face look longer from the front.

Item: Her teeth were all right except that there was a gap between the two front ones, and for that reason none of them photographed well.

Item: Her face was rather long and diamond shaped, rather than femininely oval. The way she made herself up tended to make her face look longer than it was.

Item: Her mouth was wide, with a very full upper lip. It made her face appear heavy.

Dinah was not one to be offended at the criticisms of the cosmeticians. She was quite philosophical about it—and quite practical.

"Not being pretty really helped me at that point in my life. I never sat back and said, 'Look, I'm pretty.' Nobody ever told me I was. So I had always worked on my appearance."

Even when she was growing up she had experimented with makeup, sending away for any product advertised in the magazines that promised instant beauty.

"I'm in your hands," she told the cosmeticians. They were the experts, and Dinah always believed in letting experts make decisions in areas where she was not expert.

The first thing the beauty technicians did was to bleach her black hair honey-blonde. Then they restyled it so that it was not in a pompadour but in a shape that tended to make her face look shorter rather than longer. Also, the rats and falls went onto the trash heap.

The second thing they did was to give her a light golden foundation makeup to balance out her naturally dark skin tone. This base tended to fool the camera enough so that her face did not photograph dark.

Over the golden foundation they put on a rosy-toned secondary foundation, to give her face the proper flesh tones. On top of that went a *light* dusting of powder. "It took me a while to learn that too much makeup, especially a lot of powder, is aging," Dinah said.

The powder, incidentally, was used to set the makeup for the long working day in front of the cameras. On top of that, they put a rose-colored matte-finish rouge over her cheekbones and nose.

The third thing they did was to accentuate her dark-brown eyes by applying a thin line of taupe liquid eyeliner to each upper lid. Her eyes were her best feature, the taupe eyeshadow brought them out into full

view. Her eyebrows were restructured to give her face a
softer roundness and accentuate her eyes.

The cosmeticians then put Dinah in the hands of
plastic surgeons for work on her nose. It was shortened
and restructured so that it would no longer dominate
her face.

Fifth, she was sent to a dental surgeon who capped
all her teeth in such a way that there was no longer a gap
between the two front ones. "They like to killed me,"
Dinah told a columnist later. "They filed my teeth and
put on caps, they angled my eyebrows, they dyed my
hair."

There was little more that needed to be done. The
shape of her face could be handled by the new hairstyle
her hairdresser had evolved, and the shape of her lips
could be helped a great deal by the dental work on her
teeth.

When they were through with her, she was an entirely different young woman, and oddly enough, a
woman who on the outside resembled more perfectly the
woman that had always been inside. It was a miracle of
cosmetic technology over nature.

She was not unhappy with the outcome. In those
days such cosmetic work was usually done in high
secrecy. In fact, a "nose bob" was something that no
one discussed in polite company. Certainly it was not
the kind of thing that got into the newspapers. But
Dinah never kept it a secret.

"Dinah Shore," newspaperman John Lester wrote
later, "was among the first of the big names to
recognize that Mother Nature isn't always right and to
take definite steps to improve on her original handi-
work." She was never too sensitive to admit it.

And so it was that sometime in 1942, a girl with a
dark complexion, jet black hair, a gaptoothed mouth,
and a long-nosed face became a golden girl with honey
blonde hair, straight teeth, a short nose, and a sunny
look that had never been hers before.

Press agents could now brag about her statistics: She was 5 feet 6 inches in height, 110 pounds, and had a waistline of 21 inches—"the smallest in radio." She had brown eyes, a large full mouth, and blonde hair "worn long and fluffy to give warmth and width to a classically proportioned long oval face. And her lips are as red as nature and lipstick can make them. She is the most vividly alive creature in all Radio Town."

The stunning change did not go unnoticed by her friends of former years.

"She changed her hair from brunette to blonde," said one of her friends in Nashville. "And she changed her appearance drastically. She must have had plastic surgery. She certainly had her nose fixed. She actually looked beautiful!"

Another girl friend said: "I wouldn't have recognized her if I had met her on the street. There had been an incredible change in her appearance."

But all her friends agreed that if her outward appearance had changed, that fierce inner glow and her marvelous personality were exactly the same.

And her outward appearance changed just in time. Dinah was in love again—but this time it was the real thing. She had fallen for an actor—a handsome leading man who was engaged to Hedy Lamarr, one of the most beautiful women in motion pictures. How could Dinah Shore compete with the beautiful Hedy unless she herself was beautiful?

4

Breakfast
at the
Failing Elk

George Montgomery grew up on a 2,000-acre ranch near Brady, Montana, a tiny town near Great Falls. Born there on August 29, 1916, he was the youngest of fifteen children.

His name at birth was not actually "George Montgomery," any more than Dinah's name at birth was "Dinah Shore." George was born with a different surname. His full name was George Montgomery Letz. His parents were both born in Sevastopol, Russia, in the Crimea, and they emigrated to the United States in 1913 with their brood of children.

George grew up handling real down-to-earth farm chores: herding cattle, plowing fields, harvesting grain, digging ditches and post holes, and doing almost everything else involved in cattle raising and general farm work.

Getting to school was no easy matter; he and his brothers and sisters frequently tramped six to eight miles through snow in the winter to get there.

When George was a very little boy, his brothers and sisters earned themselves a motion picture projector by selling magazines door-to-door. Movies were a new fad then, but there were no theaters near the Letz spread.

They converted an old barn into a motion picture house and charged admission to neighborhood kids to see short reels of silent movies. To them, motion pictures were theater, even though most of the films they showed were pretty well chewed up by the time they got them threaded into their clap-trap projector.

Yet the crude and incredibly jerky pictures that moved intrigued George Letz. When he was in the fourth grade, a teacher asked him: "What do you want to be when you grow up?"

George thought about the flickering pictures he had seen in the barn and blurted out: "I want to be an actress!" The teacher hastily corrected his grammatical gender, but remembered what he had said. Later, when *Rebecca of Sunnybrook Farm* was presented as the class play, she gave him a small part in it.

After graduation from high school, George enrolled at the University of Montana. He had always liked carpentry work around the ranch, so he signed up for the architectural course. One of his older brothers was already a civil engineer. George liked to build things and work with his hands.

In his freshman year, his broad shoulders and muscular build won him the heavyweight boxing championship of the campus. Unfortunately, he had begun college in the depths of the Great Depression, and his money ran out at the end of his first year. He dropped out to return to the ranch.

For a few months he played semi-pro baseball, but

the team went broke and that chance folded. Cow-punching didn't pay well at all. The family ranch was in financial trouble because there were so many mouths to feed.

The Letz brothers left for different parts of the country. Michael, the civil engineer, wound up out on the West Coast. He had gone through college and had a good profession. But he had the same trouble that other civil engineers were having at the time: There were no jobs to be had.

He wrote back home to George that Los Angeles was a fine place to live, and George worked his way out there. Unfortunately, he found that jobs were as scarce as hen's teeth, exactly the way they had been back home in Montana. But he managed to find work in a bar, mixing drinks.

Up to that time, George had never touched a drop of liquor. Nor did he, even after his stint behind the counter.

"I thought a 'zombie' was a dead man walking," he told a friend later. Nevertheless he did a tolerable job as a barkeep. He was a handsome, six-foot-three, two-hundred-pound muscular he-man. And he had a mild, gentle, Western way about him.

He made friends with everybody who came into the bar. Some of them began telling him about the movie business, which was one industry that was really booming at the time. People wanted entertainment that was cheap, and dreams of happiness to cling to. Lots of people were getting jobs working for the movies.

"You're a big strong handsome guy, George. You ought to take a crack at it."

"I can't act," George pointed out.

"Hell, you can ride," someone observed.

Soon after that conversation, one of the studios put out a call for horseback riders to work in a Greta Garbo picture. George Letz showed up at the casting of-fice and landed a job as a Cossack cavalryman. He and thirty other out-of-work cowpokes rode up and down the San Fernando Valley gulches raising dust and shaking the earth while the star and her entourage played out their parts in front of the cameras.

After that was over, George found himself a job as a movie stunt man, riding a horse and acting as a double for a cowboy star. George's first stunt was to ride the action scenes for *The Lone Ranger*. In a mask, even his family in Brady couldn't recognize him.

He began to pick up odd jobs at Republic Studios, doubling for he-men actors—fighting, jumping off roofs, running and riding through fires and rivers, shooting Indians. It was part-time work at best, and he made little money.

Disgusted, he went back to Montana. Meanwhile, his brother Michael had left California for South America. Three weeks after George had returned to Brady, Michael gave him a call from Los Angeles. He was back and was soon heading for San Francisco. He wanted to see George.

George hitchhiked out and had a few days with his brother. This time he decided to stay a little longer, and got a job painting and decorating a place that would open as a nightclub, using his talent at carpentry and painting to make a living. He had four weeks of that, and then the job ended.

He made the rounds of the bars again, and signed on at the Bublichki. It was at the Bublichki that he ran into a brassy aggressive little guy by the name of Benny Medford. Medford was an actor's agent.

"You're a tall, handsome guy, George. I can get you a job in the movies. But that name stinks."

"What name?" George was offended.

"Letz. It sound awful. Drop it. You're George Montgomery."

And he was.

Medford wasn't all hot air. He sold George Montgomery, minus the Letz, to Twentieth-Century Fox. The brass took one look at the screen test, saw a tall, virile, and almost beautiful hunk of manhood, and couldn't resist.

Director Ray McCarey was assigned to whip the new discovery into a passable actor. McCarey led George into the studio screening room and made him watch scores of Gary Cooper movies. "Don't copy him," he warned George. "Just be as natural as he is, and you'll be fine."

George watched, studied, tried out for some parts, and got signed on for a series of Westerns. The studio publicity department sent out news releases saying that Fox was allocating $5,900,000 for films to star George Montgomery in the very near future. The sum was a huge figure in those days, proving that the front office was very high on their Montana-born discovery.

George was scheduled to make four Zane Grey pictures in the first several years of his contract. He did make two of them. Then he was assigned to several straight dramas.

Actually, his Westerns weren't bad pictures at all. In the book *The Western*, a critique on the Western film, George N. Fenin and William K. Everson mentioned his first two pictures, *Riders of the Purple Sage* and *The Last of the Duanes*, saying they were "both good, with George Montgomery."

But bigger things were in the offing, and soon George was starred in *The Cowboy and the Blonde*, a contemporary movie, opposite an actress named Mary Beth Hughes.

The picture was a spoof on Hollywood. In it, George came to Hollywood as an ex-cowpuncher, was tried out in a number of different types of roles—pirate, gangster, drawing-room comedian, collegian, musketeer, oil rigger—and finally made a hit when he was cast as—what else?—a cowboy!

Later George became Betty Grable's leading man in a picture called *Coney Island*. George Letz had never

even *been* to Coney Island! Then he played opposite
Ginger Rogers in *Roxie Hart*, a remake of *Chicago*.
George had never been to Chicago, either.

According to the gossip columns, George Montgomery began squiring a number of very important actresses around to the Hollywood night spots: Marlene
Dietrich, Greer Garson, and Ginger Rogers. These were
arranged for publicity stories.

Then, in December, 1941, just after Pearl Harbor,
George want to a tennis party given by Fred MacMurray
at his home in Beverly Hills. There he met a young 26-
year-old actress who had made a sensation in the German motion picture *Ecstasy*. She was Hedy Lamarr, actually Hedwig Eva Marie Kiesler. Hedy had already
been married twice, once at the age of sixteen to Fritz
Mandl, the German producer of *Ecstasy*, and again in
Hollywood to writer Gene Markey. Both marriages had
ended in divorce.

The tennis party was rained out and became an in-
door get-together. George sat around and talked to a
number of people. Afterward, he drove home through
the driving rain, only to find a car stalled on the road
ahead of him.

It was Hedy's car. He pushed her to a shelter, and
they started talking while he tinkered with the car to dry
off the spark plugs. The meeting was right out of a
movie script: they "met cute," in the contemporary
Hollywood phrase.

Things moved fast for George and Hedy after that.
They went everywhere together. Columnists wrote copy
about them. Tongues clacked. Gossips buzzed. On
March 24, 1942, they announced their engagement.

George was quoted: "When I first met Fred Mac-
Murray, I learned that Hedy sometimes came to his
house. And I said to myself, now I'll get to meet her!"

When asked specifics about the date of the
proposed wedding, both George and Hedy were non-

committal. "It will be as soon as we both can get enough time off to have a honeymoon," George said. "It would be a quiet wedding," Hedy said demurely. In the jargon of Hollywood, that meant they would elope to Las Vegas.

"We plan to live in Hedy's canyon home," George said. Hedy had rented it just after her divorce from Markey. As Markey's wife, she had adopted a three-year-old boy. The boy and Hedy's mother, Mrs. Gertrude Kiesler, would live there with the newlyweds. It was all very romantic.

But—enter Dinah Shore.

Among the many singing engagements Dinah Shore had in 1942 was one at the Steel Pier in Atlantic City, New Jersey. A then little-known comedian named Milton Berle was the master-of-ceremonies for the show. It was a tiring gig—she had eight or nine shows a day.

Her dressing room was so small and so drafty that she took to going out along the pier and wandering in to watch the movies that were playing at an adjoining theater. She had always been a move buff, and it was a good way to indulge in her favorite hobby.

One of the pictures interested her in an exceptionally personal way. It was a vapid story about a would-be actor from a ranch who went to Hollywood to be a movie star. The story was entirely forgettable. The actor who played the cowboy was not.

His name, she found as she read it on the list of players, was George Montgomery. He looked exactly like a cowboy should look—tall, clean-cut, handsome, muscular, masculine. He was obviously a man of few words. And he spoke in an authentic Western drawl—at least, what Dinah Shore, who knew a drawl when she heard one, considered authentic. She couldn't get him out of her mind. And she kept going to see the picture.

Her roommate, a girl in the show, saw her coming

back one night and kidded her about it. "That's a terrible picture. I saw you come out of that movie house again this afternoon. What gives?"

Dinah just smiled.

"Come on, Dinah! Why do you keep seeing that corny movie?"

"I'm studying a very special man. The leading man."

"What's so special about him?"

"That's the man I'm going to marry. George Montgomery."

"Do you know him?"

"Not yet," Dinah confessed. "But someday I will meet him."

"And then you'll ask him to marry you?" her roommate asked incredulously.

Dinah just smiled a secret smile.

Several days later her roommate threw a fan magazine on a chair next to Dinah.

"I think you'd better read that."

"What's in it?"

"There's an article about the man you're going to marry. George Montgomery."

"What's it say?"

"He's going to get married—to another woman."

Dinah picked up the magazine and leafed through it. She found the story immediately. It said that George Montgomery had just become engaged to Hedy Lamarr. And Dinah knew that Hedy Lamarr was one of the most glamorous women in Hollywood. She stared at the picture and at the caption and laid the magazine down. She didn't seem particularly affected. "I feel sorry for her."

"Who?"

"Hedy Lamarr."

"Why be sorry for Hedy Lamarr?"

"Because she intends to be married to George Montgomery. And that's one wedding that just won't take place."

She meant it. She wasn't teasing her roommate. In fact, she told another show girl about Montgomery and how she intended to marry him. The friend later said:

"You'd never think it to look at her, but Dinah Shore is as tough as steel underneath that sweet-talking, silky exterior. She gave me the eeriest feeling when she told me about George Montgomery and the fate she had reserved for him. Here he was three thousand miles away—and yet she *knew* she was going to meet him. Somehow, she was convinced that she could make it happen! And, you know, I believed her."

Shortly after her stint in Atlantic City was over, Dinah was summoned to Hollywood where she signed the bright new contract with Warner Brother Studios. Now she was closer to the man of her dreams, but Hollywood was a big place and there wasn't much chance to meet him.

If you weren't Dinah Shore, that is, there wasn't much chance. Distance didn't stop Dinah at all, or even slow her down. She simply waited for the opportunity she knew would come.

The opportunity to see him in the flesh came rather quickly. She was signed on for a special show at the Shrine Auditorium in Los Angeles. Bing Crosby was standing at Dinah's side, peering through a hole in the curtain, counting the audience.

The handsome Montanan came sauntering down the theater aisle with a tall, good-looking young woman named Kay Williams on his arm.

Dinah turned to Bing. "You know who that man is?" she asked him.

Bing said, "Sure. That's George Montgomery."

"Wrong. That's the man I'm going to marry." Dinah peeked through the curtain again. "Gosh, he certainly knows a lot of beautiful women."

The unshakable Bing Crosby was a little bit shaken by Dinah's aplomb. He peered out and then frowned at Dinah.

"You know him?"

"I know him, but he doesn't know me."

"Then how do you figure to work this out?"

"Want to help?" Dinah asked with a big smile.

"Don't get me mixed up in your one-woman campaign, Dinah!" Bing pleaded. "I'm no marriage broker."

Dinah tried to cajole him a little, but he absolutely wouldn't be cajoled. "I've always got a lot of sweet-talk on hand if I want it," Dinah recalled later. "But for some reason I couldn't sweet-talk Bing into helping."

"If I had any sense," Crosby continued, "I'd go and warn George of what he's liable to get into if he doesn't watch out!"

Bing later told a friend: "That Dinah Shore gal is something else. She may look like cotton candy wouldn't melt in her mouth. But she knows what she wants, and she's harder than flint about getting it. I'd sure hate to be the man she set her sights on! Poor George."

Her meeting with her husband-to-be, although he didn't know that was what he was, occurred soon after that.

"I don't want to sound mystical," Dinah wrote later, "but twice I was sure I'd meet George Montgomery before I actually did."

The first time was during an appearance at a Gershwin Concert in the Hollywood Bowl.

"This was the first time my extrasensory perception went into action," Dinah recounted. "I was so sure I'd see George there that I stood behind the curtain, where I could peer at the audience. Sure enough, there came George.

"He seemed a little surprised when we were introduced," Dinah wrote.

George took one careful look at her and said, "I thought you were one of Eddie Cantor's child prodigies! Now I can see you're not fourteen—and I'm glad."

That comment was nourishment for Dinah for

weeks. The meeting also proved the fact that her extrasensory perception was just as accurate as it had been when it had warned her of her mother's death when she was going on sixteen.

Toward the end of the year, the Hollywood Canteen was ready to open up. Along with hundreds of other stars, Dinah was on hand to help out. She drifted about being friendly and open with everybody. Actually, she was looking over the crowd to see if she could spot George Montgomery. She couldn't find him on opening night.

Night after night she returned to the Canteen.

Then one evening, when she was dressing for her night at the Canteen, she *knew* he would be there that night.

"My ESP tipped me off a second time when I was dressing for the Hollywood Canteen. I was so positive I would meet my crush again that I told my roommate, 'I'm going to meet George Montgomery tonight.' "

And she did.

In her own words, Dinah recalled the meeting: "Al Melnick, the agent, was at the door of the Canteen when I arrived.

" 'Who's here tonight?'

" 'Oh—Marlene Dietrich, John Garfield, George Montgomery . . .'

" 'Montgomery? Gee, he's cute—where is he?' And there was George eating a ham sandwich. We had our first date that night and neither of us dated anyone else again. Before he said good night he arranged to meet me the next morning. I remember he showed up with a bunch of violets."

George was a Corporal in the Army Signal Corps at the time, serving in the First Motion Picture Division, waiting assignment. One of their dates was ice skating on a frozen rink in Westwood Village. Dinah had grown up in magnolia land, but she had learned to skate—a legacy of her athletic mother.

As George was tightening her ice skates for her he saw that her right foot was different from her left. The arch was higher, due to the fact that many years of exercise had given it a higher instep.

"It looks like you broke your foot at one time," George commented casually as he worked at her skate lace.

Dinah turned pale. Panic welled within her. She had thought she was cured of her sensitivity about the fact that she had been crippled by polio. She didn't want to admit it—not to this man!

"Yes," she said hastily. "That's it. I broke it."

George continued to lace up the skate, but now Dinah was trembling and felt almost sick.

"What's the matter?" he asked, genuine concern on his face.

The one thing that Dinah could not do was tell a lie—even a little white lie. It was totally against her nature. She knew that she was deceiving the man she loved. She couldn't allow him to believe something about her that wasn't true.

"I—I didn't break my foot. I had polio when I was a little girl!" She blurted it out and was almost in tears.

"Here, here!" George cried. "What's the matter with you?"

"I didn't want to tell you."

"Why not?" He had her in his arms and was comforting her.

"You're so healthy. You grew up in the outdoors. You're strong and wouldn't ever have polio. I was afraid it would make a difference." She was shamefaced now, but terrified in her heart at what his reaction would be to her childhood weakness.

He looked at her, a slow smile lighting up his face. "Back home in Montana, Dinah, we sometimes shoot crippled horses. But we practically *never* shoot crippled people!"

Dinah burst out laughing, dried her tears, and skated off with him.

After several more dates, Dinah asked him cautiously about Hedy Lamarr. After all, the two of them were still engaged.

"Oh, she's fine," George said.

"Do you ever go out anymore?"

George looked at her with amusement. "I think she's going out with someone else."

"But, your engagement—" She caught herself and put her hand over her mouth.

"I guess it's kind of fizzled out," George grinned.

"I hope she's very happy with her other man," said Dinah softly.

George laughed out loud. "Me, too."

Things were marching along in fantastic style, Dinah thought. There was no need to pretend any longer, no need to maneuver, no need to entice George with sweet-talk.

Then the blow fell. Uncle Sam was the dealer. George was ordered to Alaska.

Alaska! That was somewhere almost on the other side of the moon. Dinah had to get out an atlas to find out where he was headed. She determined to keep cheerful about his departure, although she was more upset than he was.

They had a date. Dinah drove George in her car to a small Italian restaurant in the Valley. There the two of them drank wine and ate by candlelight. Afterward, they drove far out past Ventura until they were once again on the Coast Route. They parked the car and stood on an outcrop of land, listening to the Pacific Ocean break at their feet.

It was goodbye.

But no proposal.

One day George took off quite suddenly. That was it. Dinah got letters from him from on board a ship, and then from his APO number. Once away from civilization, George found himself thinking more and more about Dinah. He began to wonder why he had neglected to ask her to marry him.

In fact, his buddies took him to task. They liked George, but they couldn't believe what a prize jerk he was! "You let a real live one like Dinah Shore get away from you?" one buddy asked him in astonishment. They all told him the same thing, in no uncertain terms.

George finally began putting some of his thoughts down on paper in his letters home. Dinah wrote right back to him, kidding him along. That was all.

"I have said kiddingly on occasion, 'I snagged my man,' but I really never used any aggressive techniques," she said. "Oh, I might have hinted in one or two letters that I was dating another actor—but it's fair to use such feminine wiles in the game of love, isn't it?"

Fair or not, George got the message. He went moodily around camp, wondering what Dinah was doing right at that moment, and visions of civilian Adonises running all over Hollywood with her assailed him, putting him off his feed and making him feel like a lovesick cow.

"How's it going with Dinah Shore?" his buddies kept asking him everytime he got a letter. He didn't tell them she was running around with every eligible bachelor in Southern California.

He sat around camp at night on pins and needles, wondering what to do about it. Finally he got up his nerve and proposed to her by V-mail.

Then he waited, almost literally holding his breath, for her answer. None came. Even his buddies were upset by Dinah's treachery. The theory bruited about camp was that she had run off with some other guy and George would have to read about it the papers.

George's state of mind was worse than that of a GI who had just gotten a "Dear John" letter from an errant spouse or fiancée. Why didn't Dinah write and say she would marry him?

As a matter of fact, her letters kept coming. They mentioned dates she was having, they mentioned other actors, they mentioned GI's she had met at the Hollywood Canteen.

Her letters mentioned nothing about marriage. George sulked. He stopped writing.

Dinah wondered why he didn't write, and she wrote to him to upbraid him for not writing. He couldn't figure out what to do now. Whatever he did was wrong.

Suddenly orders came through. George was to be shipped back to Los Angeles for reassignment. He didn't even have time to write.

Once in town, he hurried over to Dinah's place, the "Charm School." It was mid afternoon. George banged on the door. Dinah answered and stood there staring dumbly at him.

"George," she said stupidly.

"Yes! Why didn't you write *yes*?" George yelled.

Dinah was stunned. "Yes, what?"

"Yes, you'll marry me?"

"You never asked." Dinah was trying hard not to have the vapors like any good Southern girl would at the prospect of a hysterical love scene like the one she was playing.

"I proposed by V-mail!" George shouted.

"I accept in person!" Dinah retorted, holding out her arms to him.

"It's about time!"

Clinch.

"Let's get married today," George said once they had disentangled themselves from one another. Members of the Charm School were standing around in the background with their mouths open and their ears straining.

"I can't," Dinah said sensibly.

"Why not?"

"I'm too busy."

"Too busy to get married?" George was shouting again.

"I've got a 'Command Performance' show this afternoon," said Dinah, enumerating the points on her fingers. "Then there's my Spanish lesson afterward."

George stared at her, making a face. Dinah saw the joke suddenly and began to laugh. "Well, the heck with the Spanish lesson!" she said. "We'll go as soon as the show's over." And they did.

They weren't alone. All the available members of the Charm School were with them in the car. It was a beautiful night, the stars bright above the Mojave Desert. They drove across to Las Vegas, where at three A.M. they found a Justice of the Peace on the outskirts of the town.

His name was O'Malley. Dinah had brought along a dress to be married in, but there was no place to change. O'Malley showed her an empty garage behind a tiny cottage nearby, and there she changed.

As it was, she wore a coat over her wedding dress because at three in the morning in the desert it was ice-cold!

They were married as Frances Rose Shore and George Letz. Alert photographers heard about it, or maybe some little bird at the studio had got wind of the event and had telephoned them.

"We went to an all-night joint for our wedding breakfast," Dinah recalled. "I remember the name to this day—The Failing Elk!"

They ate damp toast with margarine, warmed-over eggs, and cold coffee. "I ate heartily," Dinah said. "Then we drove back to Los Angeles and the two of us moved in with the Charm School. It was the wrong threshold—I mean, it wasn't our own place really—but George carried me over it." And that was the honeymoon.

The letter of proposal George had written was

delivered to Dinah the following afternoon. It had been shipped by mistake to Adak, a tiny island off the coast of Alaska.

They were married on December 5, 1943. Three days later Corporal George Montgomery was transferred to San Antonio, Texas.

5

A V2 Rocket
with a
Southern Accent

Dinah Shore's career was booming now. She was involved in three separate careers, in addition to that of housewife. She was a radio star with her own show, a recording star producing hit records with regularity, and a budding motion picture star.

Her fifteen-minute radio show had been expanded to a half hour in 1942. In 1943 it was named "Dinah's Open House," and ran as such through 1944.

Variety was very kind to the program. "Dinah Shore, an obscure sustaining vocalist of local New York stature only four years ago, emerges as a top name and personality for General Foods." The review went on, "Miss Shore, already recognized as a torcher, proves she has become one of the top emotional ballad singers." And, "She is a suave, assured, and warmly ingratiating M.C. She has, beyond a doubt, arrived."

In the summer of 1943, she became the hostess and featured singer for a blockbuster of a radio show called "Paul Whiteman Presents," featuring the 35-piece orchestra of the renowned jazz leader. The show was the thirty-minute replacement for the NBC network Edgar Bergen—Charlie McCarthy program on Sunday evening.

It was a high-budget variety show. Guests ranged from Eddie Cantor, George Burns and Gracie Allen, Red Skelton, Ed "Archie" Gardner, and Jimmy Durante to non-performers like Ferde Grofe, the composer, Johnny Mercer, the songwriter, and Matty Malneck, an orchestra leader.

The show got off to a fine start with guests Harry Barris, Al Rinker, and Bing Crosby, all of whom had begun with Whiteman in 1930 as a trio called "The Rhythm Boys." Although the show lasted for only thirteen weeks—from June 6 to August 29—it became a landmark in variety shows. Its success had a great deal to do with its hostess's growing mastery of that special blend of formality and informality needed to pull such a show together.

Dinah's radio appearances helped promote her records, which were selling like the proverbial hotcakes. Her records were in all the juke boxes, and her name appeared regularly on lists of "best-selling" records and in popularity polls. Her popularity with servicemen increased by leaps and bounds, helped initially by appearances in front of GI groups in the States getting ready for shipment overseas. She logged thousands of miles singing for them with entertainers like Bing Crosby, Bob Hope, and Fred Astaire.

Her third career—motion pictures—started out with a bang. She appeared with Eddie Cantor in a picture called *Thank Your Lucky Stars*. It was a mélange of entertainment fabricated strictly for the amusement and uplift of lonely GI's. As such it wasn't much of a picture, but simply a showcase to feature various singers and comedians.

Bosley Crowther of *The New York Times* criticized Cantor for creating "amateur night at the studio," but he did have kind words for Dinah. "Dinah Shore puts her throaty contralto behind 'The Dreamer,' 'How Sweet You Are,' and 'Thank Your Lucky Stars,' the title song." Years later the book *Movies on TV* categorized the picture as a "silly film containing all the Warner Brothers stars of 1943," but gave it a three star rating anyway: "Recommended for star gazers."

As a debut for a brand new singer and potential actress, it really wasn't much to rave about. Dinah was so nervous that when a sneak preview was shown in one of the Los Angeles suburbs, she drove out to the theater, but was afraid to get out of the car, and stayed all through the showing huddled alone in the parking lot. She could only be enticed to see the picture once friends had assured her that she came over very well in it.

And even then, when she finally saw herself on the giant screen, she squirmed down into her seat and covered her eyes with her hands. Then she whispered to her companion in anguished tones, "Is that a face, or a *condition*?"

Others liked her more than she liked herself, apparently. Shortly after the picture was released, she was called in for an interview with Sam Goldwyn. He wanted to put her in a motion picture with a new star he had discovered named Danny Kaye. The picture was a pretty lightweight confection about a troopship with a gaggle of nurses on board, but Goldwyn thought it would be just right for the servicemen.

The picture was called *Up in Arms* and it made a star of Danny Kaye. Crowther thought the picture was strictly second-rate. But he liked Danny Kaye. "He does one dandy jive number with Dinah Shore to 'Tess's Torch Song,' '' he wrote. "Miss Shore's connection with the picture is incidental at best. She plays an army nurse who loves the comic. But, when they let her, she sings evermore.'' He added, " 'Now I Know,' by Arlen and Koehler, is her best—and one of the year's better—songs.''

Newsweek was kinder than Crowther. It said that Dinah Shore evidenced "a flair for comedy" in the Danny Kaye outing.

Hollywood was now in high gear, grinding out potpourries of dancing, singing, and joking. Dinah's next assignment was in *Follow the Boys*, made at Universal, and starring George Raft and Vera Zorina, with Charles Grapewin, Grace McDonald, Charles Butterworth, and the usual "cast of thousands."

A thin story about the Hollywood Victory Committee (in reality the U.S.O., which was set up to help win the war by entertainment and morale building), *Follow the Boys* was more of the same. Dinah sang three numbers: "I'll Get By," "I Walk Alone," and "Mad About Him Blues," Even W. C. Fields, who did his fantastically successful poolroom skit, was in it, along with Orson Welles, and everyone anybody could think of. "It makes for cheap entertainment and is hardly a tribute to the players it presents," Crowther grumbled.

Dinah's first three pictures were typical of the wartime formula pictures pouring out of Hollywood. The recipe was simple: cram as much singing, dancing, and comedy as possible into two hours of film, regardless of plot. Also get a large batch of big-name entertainers to make the billboards look good.

Using Dinah Shore as a singer with a few lines to say didn't give her much chance to learn how to act in front of the cameras. As usual, the Hollywood moguls were taking the easy way out, trying to get maximum big-name clout with feeble material. The musical genre of which her three pictures were an example gave rise to the memorable press agent's line always added at the end of the sales pitch: ". . . and a cast of thousands."

Dinah Shore's fourth picture, made for International Pictures and released by RKO-Radio, was called *Belle of the Yukon*. The stars were Randolph Scott and Gypsy Rose Lee. Dinah Shore was given third billing, attesting to her popularity on radio, before the troops, and in the nation's juke boxes. Other supporting players were Bob Burns, Charles Winninger, and Robert Armstrong.

It was a story of the Gold Rush days in the Klondike, involving the efforts of "Honest" John Calhoun, a confidence artist, to go straight. With the appearance of an old flame from his past, his love affair with the singing star of his dance hall turns into a thorny little triangle.

The problem with the picture was that it didn't know whether it was satire or drama. As such, it wavered between humor and tragedy, with no one—not even the actors—knowing how to play it.

"Other developments—a romance between Dinah Shore and a piano player, a bank robbery, and a few mistaken identities—have been included in the labyrinthine scenario," Bosley Crowther noted.

"Miss Shore does well by several [numbers], the best of which are 'Sleigh Ride in July,' and 'Like Someone in Love,' both of which have a vogue on the radio. . . . Despite its technicolor glitter, *Belle of the Yukon* yields few nuggets. It's fool's gold, after all."

In spite of the big strides she was making in radio and on the juke boxes, and the faltering advances she was making in her motion picture career, the most important thing in Dinah's life in those years just after her marriage to Corporal George Montgomery was the entertainment of American servicemen.

She was virtually indefatigable in her appearances. Quite soon she became the Number One Sweetheart of the Service; or at least, she was one of the many singers and actresses who were vying with each other for the honor.

But her attitude was just right for the GI's who listened to her sing. "I'm just small-town, middle-class, and I like everybody. I'm a ham about singing and I'll sing to the servicemen until their last breath."

One GI summed her up: "She's got the kind of voice you'd like to take home to your mother."

Her popularity was zooming dramatically. She got letters by the bundle from overseas—about 5,000 a week, in fact, most of them from servicemen. She answered every one of them with the help of her secretary.

Typical of the letters she got was one sent from Sicily during the 1943 invasion.

"Dear Miss Shore:

"Living in an olive grove on a hillside in the interior of Sicily are three members of the United States Air Force who are among your most ardent admirers. We have one of your records and it has become such a favorite with us that we decided we should write to express our feeling of appreciation to you. The record is 'I Look at Heaven,' and 'I Can't Give You Anything But Love, Baby.'

"In the evening we sit in the darkness of the nightly blackout and listen to you sing. It brings home, sweethearts, families, and old friends right into the heart of Sicily. We thought you might be interested to know how we three treasure your lone record, which is hardly ever in our album, but always on the phonograph. Lord help the fellow who breaks it.

Gratefully—————————"

* * *

Dinah's performing schedule included many service hospitals all around the country. She would go into a hospital and sing a solo at the bedside of each man, spending hours in the process.

After Dinah had sung about a dozen solos at the hospital in Victorville Army Flying Camp, a large complex located out in the middle of the Mojave Desert, Bob Hope shook his head in admiration. "First time," he said, "I ever saw a juke box on legs!"

She sang for the sailors at the Presidio in San Francisco one evening, and as one of the officers was escorting her to her car after the performance, she noticed a number of sailors wearing arm bands marked "S.P."

"What does S.P. mean?" she asked.

"Shore Patrol," the officer replied.

"My," she exclaimed, "that was awfully sweet of you, but you shouldn't have gone to all that trouble just for me!"

There were some poignant moments, too. Dinah visited Rhoads General Hospital in Utica, New York, which was ministering to 3,600 wounded servicemen. She sang for groups of men, for men confined to beds, for everyone working there.

Ticker Freeman, her accompanist, was picking up his lead sheets as Dinah walked away from one group, when he saw an infantryman with a shattered leg watching her go. "Brother," he said, tears glistening in his eyes, "you sure can't help lovin' a gal like that!"

One day she sang at two Naval and Marine base hospitals. Her singing took eleven hours, during which she finished a record number of 157 songs.

Later, at the Santa Ana Replacement Center in Southern California near Los Angeles, she sang to the men for three hours. At the end of her performance, one of the GI's called out, "Ain't you got a kiss for me? I'm a rebel like you all."

"Sure," said Dinah, and, fast on her feet, kissed

him quickly and ran. The soldier's sergeant put him on guard duty that night.

"You won't be able to sleep anyhow," he told him. "Wait until your girl down South hears about it. Will she ever understand?"

At a Marine base, the Marines teased her at the end of her performance into giving one man a kiss for them all. Dinah, thinking of another quick exit, kissed the first one she got to in the front row, and then fled up the aisle.

Unfortunately she had kissed the wrong man. He was the only soldier in an audience made up of Marines! She was still running when she heard the roar that went up and learned why.

"It'll spur them on to finish the war quickly," she observed, "so they can come back and hang me."

At the Kaisar Shipyards, where she was entertaining the blue-collar workers who built ships and were launching a new warship, she accidentally spilled a whole bottle of launch champagne on Bing Crosby's newest—and loudest—Hawaiian shirt.

"This is one time, Dinah," Crosby said through a frozen smile, "that I'd be glad to give you the shirt right off my back!"

Dinah Shore records were being played all over the world now. When sailors on a certain destroyer in the South Pacific played her records, they called it their "Shore Leave"!

Her popularity wasn't limited to Yanks, either. The Royal Air Force squadron stationed at Dyce Field, Aberdeen, Scotland, rationed Dinah's music to the troops. The outfit had only one of her records, and limited its play to three times a day. When it was on, everyone crowded around for a "Dinah Break."

One night Dinah met a flyer at the Hollywood apartment when she and her roommates gave a party for servicemen. After he went overseas to take part in the invasion of North Africa, she received V-mail letters from him, and wrote letters answering him with regularity. On May 18, 1943, he wrote to her, from "somewhere in Africa," the following letter:

> *"Dear Dinah:*
>
> *"Thank you so much for your letter dated April 16. I think of you often and of the wonderful time I had at your house that night. We have a B-26 named after you here. I am on the crew so that is how it received the title 'Dinah Shore.'*
>
> *"The fellows asked me the next time I wrote to ask you to send us a big picture of yourself to put in the plane. The ship has already been on several missions, in fact more than you can count on your fingers.*
>
> *"She always comes back. She had a few scars from the battles she has seen so far. I will put a little bomb on the picture for your scrapbook. Well, I've got to go now—thanks again for your letter.*
>
> *Affectionately, your friend————. "*

Dinah sent the picture, and a letter, but received no answer confirming its recipt. Months later she got a letter from the flyer's mother, who lived in Indiana.

> *"Dear Miss Dinah Shore:*
>
> *"I am writing this letter to tell you that my son, ——, has been missing in action since August 4. He often told me how very nice you had been to him and I have your picture you gave him. He sent it to me when he left to keep until his return. He wrote me he had named his plane after you. Our last letter*

*was dated July 25. I want to thank you for being so
kind to him. It did make him so happy and I want
you to know I think it was very dear of you.*

Sincerely, Mrs. ———."

After that heartbreaker, Dinah resolved to get
overseas herself to sing to the troops where they were
fighting, rather than over short-wave radio or through
recordings.

While her orders were in the works in Washington,
the Army Air Corps gave the George Letzes a surprise:
Corporal George Montgomery Letz was shipped home
from Alaska, where he was serving with the Combat
Photographic Unit, for a short furlough.

Dinah took a brief leave herself, and the two went
on a delayed honeymoon to Montana, where they
dropped in on the Letz clan. It was one of the most
idyllic times in Dinah's life. The scenery around the
place was magnificent. The family was large and interesting. And George was relaxed and fun to be with.

While they were there, the cook was suddenly taken
sick. Dinah started out her marriage cooking breakfast
pork chops for a dozen ranch hands, in addition to the
entire Letz family. "By the time the dishes were
washed," she said, "they came in for lunch, and when
those were dried and stacked, they were back for
dinner!"

She kept following George around taking pictures
of him. She had resumed her old hobby of photography. With George, she couldn't resist snapping the
shutter at him. "He's so beautiful, I just have to keep
taking his picture!" she said later.

She loved his family. She met all the brothers and
sisters who were still living at home, and Mr. and Mrs.
Letz.

They went horseback riding and played baseball
with the Letz clan. It was a rough game. The Letz girls

were not dainty. The Letz men were roustabouts. Dinah twisted her ankle—sprained it, actually. It had to be bandaged up so she could walk. "Don't you think my husband is sweet?" she told everyone. "I sprained my ankle, and he didn't shoot me."

Bride and groom rode up into the boondocks and bought a 20,000 acre spread to use for a hideaway later on. All too soon the time ran out and George was on his way back to the war.

Shortly after that, Dinah's overseas orders came through. She was to make a two-month tour of England and France, where American troops were pushing back Hitler's army.

She told friends, "I've wanted to go for so long, I'm looking forward to the trip being the greatest experience of my life. It's going to be wonderful to see personally so many of the boys who have written to me."

She had never been out of the United States; it was going to be a new thrill for her. The newspapers took the tour in stride. "Allies Hurl Second Secret Weapon at Germans—Dinah Shore—An Allied V-2," said one headline, a favorite of Dinah's.

Ticker Freeman had never been out of the States, either. "He'd never even left Paterson, New Jersey, until I got him to go to Hollywood," Dinah laughed. "But he wants to go abroad."

Army technicans rebuilt an old spinet piano, condensing it down into a 60-pound miniature, making it a lot easier for the men to haul around in the field. And Ticker was ready to leave.

The troupe flew first to London, where Dinah met Major General Jimmy Doolittle, head of the U.S. Air Force in Britain. The General gallantly took Dinah Shore for an outing on the River Thames.

"He was a terrible punter," Dinah recalled. "Actually, punting is just pushing yourself along with a big pole. But the General didn't know how to do it. He kept rocking the boat. It was just luck we weren't dunked in the Thames."

In London, Dinah and Ticker worked with Special Services putting together a propaganda program for broadcast to Germany over the Allied shortwave underground radio system.

She crooned *Der Mann Den Ich Liebe* ("The Man I Love"), learning it in phonetic German, which she sang with a Nashville, Tennessee, drawl. "It should only happen to the Germans!" she laughed.

After the music was over, she became a "Tokyo Rose" in reverse, reading carefully written "messages" to the wives of German soldiers waiting at home for their husbands to come back.

"The war is drawing to a close," she told them in her hillbilly German. "It would be wise to surrender now. Then you will see your loved ones quickly. If you wait much longer, you will never see them again. It is a very simple thing to surrender. I urge you to do so."

Unfortunately, the Germans didn't heed her advice. "Maybe my accent bothered them," said Dinah.

But the best was yet to come—the singing tour through France, where the troops were moving against Hilter's stubbornly retreating army. Dinah got very close to the men in the field. She lived the same way they did, if a little better protected.

"The most fascinating part of the trip was going through France," she recalled. "Normandy looked a lot like Tennessee, with rolling hills and hedges. They call them 'hedge rows' in France."

Five minutes after her arrival on French soil, she found herself standing on a landing craft singing to the GI's around her. She had her hair done up in a long pageboy bob. It soon began to rain, and the rain continued most of the time she was there. She could do nothing about her appearance. "I looked a fright," she confessed.

As a singer, she had always pampered her voice,

never going out in the wet weather, getting to bed early every night for a good rest, and always keeping cough drops around to soothe her throat.

In France she only slept in a bed three times during the entire two months she was there, and never even *saw* a cough drop in all that time. Yet she never missed a performance!

She adopted with amazing flexibility to the field conditions in which she found herself. At the beginning of her overland trek, she traded a packet of pancake makeup she had brought for a comfortable set of army nurse fatigues, and a lipstick for some sturdy GI boots. They saved her life.

Her "glamour equipment," as she called it, consisted of a slip and a dress. She kept them in a gas-mask cover that she hung inside the truck or jeep, or over the bicycle handlebar—whatever mode of transportation she was using at the time.

For a stage, the group used a ten-ton truck. The dressing room was any improved tent or shelter. Dinah sang in forests, pastures, theaters without stages, and stages without theaters.

She munched K rations, fortified sometimes by real food. Once, when a bottle of champagne was "liberated" from the retreating Germans, the girls in the group used it to brush their teeth. Clean teeth clearly seemed to be a higher priority at the time than a drink of bubbly.

At a front-line encampment Dinah and Ticker Freeman were entertained by a group of officers after Dinah's appearance in front of the troops. There were twenty-six officers in the dining tent. Dinah met each one of them, and when she left the table forty-five minutes later, she said goodbye to every single one of them by name and rank.

"I was staggered," said Ticker. "And so were the officers. I've never seen such a fabulous memory. But then, Dinah constantly amazes me!"

Dinah was amused when she heard Ticker's comment. "What Ticker doesn't realize is that I *did* it to stagger him. It wasn't hard to remember the names —old campus politics, you know. People like to be remembered. But I have to throw Ticker once in a while or life would get pretty dull."

It wasn't at all dull. Once, close to the front with the Third Army in Germany, Dinah was singing in a field to thousands of GI's, after which she was supposed to be present at the dedication of a bailey bridge that had been thrown across the river. It was to be called the Dinah Shore Bridge in her honor.

In the midst of the activities, there was a sudden commotion, and a rifle shot. Somebody spotted a German sniper. "And what do you think that woman did?" Ticker related in astonishment. "Run for cover? No, she took out her camera and calmly photographed the sniper. She's still got the picture. She's very proud of it."

People on the trek with her said she displayed "fabulous stamina" in addition to her courage. At the end of the tour Bob Hope cracked: "Benzedrine takes Dinah Shore to stay awake."

"Don't believe it," she said. "There were times when I was so bushed I could have gone home and stayed there for the duration. But no matter how tired I was, if I dragged myself out in front of a crowd of servicemen who really wanted to hear me and I started to sing, I wasn't tired any more."

There were some funny moments, as always. She was singing an old favorite, going along very well, when her mind seemed to black out. She realized the music was playing, but she couldn't for the life of her remember what song she was singing, or what words came next. Even the tune was lost to her.

Stunned, she stood there with her mouth open, helpless. Ticker Freeman stopped, turning to her questioningly.

She could see the sea of GI faces in front of her. She could see the hillside on which they sat, green with trees in late summer. She could see the sky and the church spire of the French village over the top of the hill. Everything was clear except the words to the song.

"Guys," she said into the mike with a laugh, "I booted that one. I can't remember the words." She heard them begin to laugh. "What was I singing, anyway?"

In a lusty shout, the entire group of GI's on the side of the grassy hill called out the name of the number: "Memories!"

She broke up. And then she sang it right through.

Paris was the highlight of the entire trip through France. "Nobody will believe it," she said, "but I was able to get a bottle of Chanel Number 5 for three packs of cigarettes. Luckily, I don't smoke!"

As for the Parisian beauties, Dinah reported, "Naturally I always had expected to find French women chic and elegant, especially their figures, but I do believe that they have been riding bicycles too long." Then she added: "Nor are they so all-fired smart looking as reported in the newspapers. American girls put on their rouge neater."

But if the glamour had worn off the faces of the women during their trials and tribulations under the Germans, they had learned to needle their German conquerors in psychologically devastating ways. It was done with skill and humor—and they got away with it!

It was even too subtle for Dinah to understand at first. She noticed that none of the girls wore green dresses, and that there were no bottles of crème de menthe in the liquor stores. And no man in Paris wore a necktie of any shade of green. In fact the shops sported no green awnings.

But the *reason* escaped her. She had to ask a Parisian: "Is there any particular scarcity of green in Paris?"

"Happily, yes," responded her Parisian friend.

"Happily? I don't get it."

"We've eliminated everything green because the Parisians dislike green—to an individual."

Dinah still didn't know why.

"The German soldiers wore green uniforms, Mademoiselle Shore. We have simply erased the color from our memories."

It was a beautiful—and effective—way to remind each Parisian to ignore the Germans.

And they had another way to get back at their German conquerors. French perfume manufacturers, always skilled in coming up with new and enticing fragrances, developed a brand new scent for the German hausfraus or sweethearts back home. It was a fantastic seller, bought up and sent back home by the jugful.

The Germans never got the joke. Because of their self-appointed superiority, they believed that the only language was German, and never bothered to learn French. The sly Parisian manufacturers had labeled the perfume *L'Espoir*—"Hope!" And everybody knew what the French hoped!

The top GI brass were all in Paris. Dinah was escorted in to meet General George S. Patton. He took her to lunch, and proved to be an interesting, charismatic, and fascinating man.

"He is adored by his men," Dinah said. "And he believes in keeping himself visible during combat. When he travels from one place to another in a jeep, he takes off his goggles so the men can see him and know he's there." Dinah also had dinner with General Omar Bradley, Patton's immediate boss. She was terribly impressed by him, too.

The high point of the whole trip through France took place at the garden of Versailles just outside Paris. She, Bing Crosby, and Fred Astaire sang to some twelve thousand GI troops who were assembled there to hear the show. It was the crowning event of the whole tour.

It wasn't all fun and games, though. The specter of death hovered very close to Dinah Shore throughout the entire wartime tour of England and France. Actually, it all started in London, when her old friend, extrasensory perception, visited her briefly once again.

The troupe was put up at a hotel in a suburb of London, enough out of the way to be safe from the buzz bombs that were raining death and destruction on London at the time. It was Hitler's last gasp before his melodramatic end in the Berlin bunker, his final desperate attempt to subdue the British by a special "secret weapon."

"This hotel is safely outside the zone of the buzz bomb targets," the tour directors assured her. Yet when she slept in that room, she was uneasy. She could recall the time she had sensed that her mother was calling to her the day she had died.

"I know ESP exists," Dinah said. "We all have it. Some of us are just better at it than others." She felt that "something" was urging her to leave the hotel room. Actually, she did nothing about it, feeling that it was simply "war nerves," as anxiety was called at that time.

Nothing happened during her stay in London. By the time she had got to Paris, however, she learned the truth. It was her old friend Bing Crosby who told her. He caught up with her in Paris just before the Versailles concernt. "Dinah," he said. "I have a special bulletin for you. You know those rooms you had at the London hotel? The one that was safely out of the way of V-2 rockets?"

"Yes?" Dinah closed her eyes, guessing what was coming.

"It was just cleaned out by a buzz bomb. Zap! Nothing left."

Dinah thanked her lucky stars it had not happened when she was there. But the specter of death wasn't eliminated with that revelation. Dinah was singing for the troops up near the front lines one night, using the back of a ten-ton truck for a stage. The GI's had rigged up an electric light that worked from a gasoline generator to spot the performers. When Dinah was singing, a sniper opened fire on the encampment and barely missed her. The lights were immediately doused and a patrol went out to capture the sniper. They got him. But the show was cancelled at that moment.

Later on, when she was returning from a performance in a pasture up near the front, she heard the GI's talking about infiltrators. Apparently German troops who spoke English were donning GI uniforms, sneaking past the lines, and pretending to be Americans—killing any soldiers they could fool.

"I was good and scared," Dinah recalled. "I returned to my tent and found a sentry, who asked me to step forward to be recognized. I was glad to see there were guards around to help.

"I didn't know the password, but told him who I was. Then I wondered if I had made a dreadful mistake. He had a *funny* accent! In fact, he didn't sound at all as if he was American! Could he be a German?"

She froze there, wondering what she could do. "Then I *knew* he was a German spy and wondered what on earth I could do to defend myself if he tried to shoot me. The only weapon I carried was a flashlight. I was beginning to shake when he told me to pass. He said he recognized my name. That wasn't a good sign either. I *had* made those broadcasts to the Germans!"

Nothing happened, Dinah related.

"Next morning I saw him in the chow line and knew he was legitimate GI. We got to talking, and he explained to me, with a smile, that he was an American, but had only migrated from Norway a few years before the war started.

"But what *really* scared me and showed me what a close call I had, was his parting comment.

" 'You were lucky, Miss Shore. I really wasn't sure you were an American. I thought *you* had an accent!' "

During the performance of another show, a GI patrol spotted a sniper hiding high up in a tree. This one was a real German. He was hauled down and taken away to the POW encampment. He never got a chance to shoot anybody. When he was interrogated before internment, he said, "I was just listening to Dinah Shore sing!" He had heard her on the propaganda network and liked her voice. That was one sniper whose capture Dinah could probably have taken credit for!

In the midst of all the running around in Paris, Dinah got a letter from Corporal George Montgomery. From Alaska he had been transferred to the European Theater of Operations. He said he might be arriving in Paris soon, and would see her if she was still there.

Excited, and bubbling over with joy at hearing from her husband, Dinah ran downstairs to the lobby of the hotel where she was staying, and ran smack into —who else?—George Montgomery. He had arrived at the same time his air mail letter had come.

The reunion was a happy but brief one. He was stationed nearby for the time being, with a Signal Corps unit. It was Dinah who had to fly back to the United States.

6

"Call Me
Mrs.
Montgomery"

At the end of the war, during which, as Albert Morehead wrote, Dinah Shore was "unquestionably the favorite entertainer of ten million American fighting men," her radio and recording careers were booming, but her motion picture career was only fair-to-middling. She made three more pictures after the end of World War II, and that was all.

One, *Fun and Fancy Free*, was a Walt Dinsey feature cartoon, released by RKO-Radio in 1947. In that one she sang a bit, but there were no extended acting parts.

Shortly after that, she was signed up for a key part in a big-budget motion picture at Metro-Goldwyn-Mayer, *Till the Clouds Roll By*, a biographical extravaganza about the life of songwriter Jerome Kern.

She was up against a great deal of talent in the cast. Robert Walker played the part of the songwriter, and Judy Garland played Marilyn Miller. Lucile Bremer was in the cast, along with Van Heflin, Van Johnson, June Allyson, Cyd Charisse, and dozens of others.

It was another potpourri, with Dinah's job mostly to sing several Kern songs—no small feat at that, but a chore that gave her no chance to do any acting. There were too many singers for Bosley Crowther and the other critics to mention any by name; he referred simply to "competent Metro youngsters"—by which he meant June Allyson, Cyd Charisse, and Dinah Shore.

Dinah's last picture for Hollywood came five years later, in 1952. It was a comedy in which she had a definite part to play. Unfortunately it turned out to be a disaster. The disaster had more to do with its timing than with its quality.

Aaron Slick from Punkin' Crick was an old-fashioned, cornball play by Walter B. Hare, adapted for the screen by Claude Binyon, and unfortunately played straight. Since it was a period piece to begin with—about a city slicker who tried to part a young heroine from her land, which possibly had oil underneath it—it deserved a better fate than being played without any humour.

The cast included Alan Young, a radio comedian who had been enjoying a vogue during and just after World War II; Robert Merrill, the great opera singer, who was trying to expand his horizons; and Dinah Shore, who also deserved better.

Let Bosley Crowther take over: "Dinah Shore plays the bucolic maiden whose farm is almost taken away by the wily slicker from the city who thinks there's oil underneath the land. And Alan Young plays the yokel who is clumsy and shy at making love but smart enough to outwit the slicker and drag the errant Miss Shore back to the farm."

Even the singing didn't appeal to him. "The songs . . . woodenly delivered by Miss Shore, Mr. Young and Robert Merrill, who plays the city rascal, were hard to remember as far as the door."

Obviously it was not a memorable motion picture. Largely as a result of its lack of impact, Alan Young returned to radio and Robert Merrill to the Metropolitan Opera.

As for Dinah Shore, she was happily married, settled down in Encino out in San Fernando Valley, performing successfully on radio, and making hit records for the juke boxes. Why did she need Hollywood? It was then that she decided once and for all that she was finished with the motion picture business.

"I bombed as a movie star," she said, summing up her eight-picutre career. "I failed for a lot of reasons. The most important was that I'm not particularly photogenic."

Actually she was wrong about that—completely wrong. But seeing the rushes and the finished product frightened her. "The camera made me hollow-cheeked and unattractive," she said. "People who had liked me on radio couldn't associate the voice with what they saw."

She felt that the movies were threatening her hard-won radio following. She kept turning down picture role after picture role, afraid of what she would look like up on the big screen.

But in truth, Dinah Shore was extremely photogenic, as she was able to prove several seasons later. The problem was that her talents were not being utilized properly by the studio executives. The studios were floundering, anyway. The formula pictures of the prewar days were dead. The Golden Era of movie-making was over.

Dinah understood some of the problem. "In each film I was given parts in which my father ran an un-

savory joint while I was an ingenue daughter, so in-
nocent I scarcely knew there was a difference between
men and women.''

In further analyzing the problem of picking parts
for herself, she told Pete Martin in a *Saturday Evening
Post* interview. ''The story line of every script sent me
was like the one in my picture *Belle of the Yukon*. In it I
played a pure-as-untracked-snow girl whose father ran a
gambling house. I fell in love with a fellow who was
suspected of being something other than he was; it
doesn't matter now what. That was merely part of what
was known as 'the complications.' ''

Sighing, Dinah continued, ''I can sum the plot up
in five sentences: Girl sings to boy. Girl suspects boy is
not what he's supposed to be. Boy leaves. Girl sings
about boy. Boy comes back, and they live happily ever
after because girl was wrong about boy; he was what he
was supposed to be all the time.''

Dinah wasn't the only one unhappy with the films
she was in. So were the studio heads. However, the
front-office executives had a different version.

''There was talk,'' Dinah related, ''that I had mur-
dered quite a few films with my two snowy little hands,
all of which didn't help me land a part in the one picture
I wanted most.'' That was the coveted role of Julie in
Show Boat. It was a singing part. Dinah was perfect for
it. She was tested and the producer told her the test was
good. However, in the end they cast Ava Gardner in the
role.

''There couldn't have been a more perfect or
exquisite Julie,'' Dinah remarked. ''What does singing
matter, when you have eyes that slant upward and the
statistics thirty-eight, twenty-five, thirty-eight?''

By the time Dinah had tried for and lost the part of
Julie, she was pretty much resigned to extricating herself
completely from the movie business.

While her motion picture career was sinking for the
third time, Dinah was just getting in stride with her

recording and radio careers. Here her versatility stood her in good stead. She could sing anything from low-down blues to cute novelties to tender love-songs—and make them all stick.

During the war her presence on juke boxes all over the world was phenomenal. She had made recordings that were record breakers: "Yes, My Darling Daughter" and "Blues in the Night." These had been issued on the Victor-Bluebird label. She had been with RCA-Victor since 1938.

On January 1, 1946, Dinah suddenly switched companies and signed a contract with Columbia Recording Corporation. When the news was announced, there were many eyebrows lifted in the music business. The unflappable *Variety* even admitted "surprise."

Manie Sacks, one of Columbia Records' go-getting vice-presidents, got Dinah to change labels. Working with Henry Jaffe, who was still handling Dinah's legal and financial affairs, Manie persuaded Dinah to make the switch.

A persuasive soul, Manie had worked a deal some time earlier with Frank Sinatra, signing him to the Columbia label. Once he had Sinatra in the bag, he tried to get Bing Crosby, but Crosby decided to stay with Decca.

With Dinah signed on, Sacks rolled up his sleeves in earnest, working closely with Dinah, Ticker Freeman, and others in the Columbia Artists and Repertoire department. Their first selection for Dinah's Columbia list was a weird little novelty called "Shoo Fly Pie." Nobody gave it much of a chance. In fact, the word went out that Columbia had lost its mind.

Released in March, 1946, the Dinah Shore number climbed right into the juke boxes, and by the middle of April it was everywhere it could be. Although its career was brief, it was strong, and it sold 400,000 singles before it died.

Meanwhile, three other songs the brain trust at

Columbia chose for Dinah began to inch up in the charts. They were "The Gypsy"; "Doin' What Comes Naturally," an Irving Berlin tune from *Annie Get Your Gun*; and "For Sentimental Reasons."

By the end of 1946, each of those three records had sold 1,000,000 apiece—big numbers in those days.

By the end of 1946, with America beating its swords back into plowshares, Dinah won first place in three of *Billboard's* 1946 categories:

(1) She was named top female vocalist on disc jockey shows.
(2) She was chosen top selling female vocalist over record counters.
(3) She was chosen top female vocalist on the nation's juke boxes.

Columbia found its successful mix of Dinah's records to average about 70 percent ballads, with rhythm numbers and novelties making up the rest. Her versatility made selecting numbers for her easy.

In 1947 she had several more big hits. Her rendition of "The Anniversary Song," in competition with Al Jolson's own recording for Decca, ran over a million in sales, and later on she made "All My Love," another Jolson song borrowed from a waltz by Emil Waldteufel.

In addition, she sang duets with Frank Sinatra on two sides of a record: "My Romance" and "Tea for Two." The proceeds went to the Damon Runyon cancer fund. Between the two of them, Sinatra and Dinah outsold all the rest of Columbia's popular singers. By the middle of 1947, Dinah's total sales were well over six million records.

Her radio career was continuing, too. She had left the "Birds-Eye Open House Show," and appeared on the "Ford Radio Show" with Peter Lind Hayes. The Ford program tried out Dinah as a comedienne, and the experiment was "not a success," according to

Newsweek magazine. "Future Dinah Shore radio shows will probably concentrate on music," the story continued.

The prediction was not quite an accurate one, but that was because *Newsweek* was not thinking about an emerging communications revolution that was now only in its infancy, but that would confound a large number of experts when it finally achieved its full growth. It was called television.

No one ever entered marriage with more pluck, hope and determination than Dinah Shore. To her, it was the fulfillment of all her years of singing, dancing, and entertaining. "As a girl," she said, "singing never seemed more to me than something to fill the gap between school and marriage."

And she had certainly picked the right man to share her life. The fact that George Montgomery was her husband constantly amazed her. She truly considered herself the luckiest of women. About her husband, she once said: "The guy has no idea of how good-looking he is, and he couldn't care less. He has a terrific physique, but has never been within yards of a barbell!"

There were other pleasant surprises in store for the new bride, once the war was over and Sergeant Montgomery had been returned to civilian status.

George, as we have mentioned, was a natural builder and frustrated architectural student. Now he drew up rough plans for professional carpenters to follow, and designed and helped remodel the ranch house the newly married Montgomerys bought in Encino, a small suburb of Los Angeles far out in the San Fernando Valley. The house stood on a two-and-a-half acre spread.

"As I was growing up on my father's Montana ranch," George said, "I used to sit by the kitchen stove on those long cold winter nights and whittle on every piece of firewood that came my way. I realize now that those whittling sessions were to determine the type of house I would one day build for my wife.

"It wasn't until two years after Dinah and I were married that I took up my old hobby again. We had bought and remodeled an old ranch house that was just what we wanted, but when we came to furnishing it, we were stumped. I suppose we could have bought antiques or reproductions, but the cost was prohibitive, and also we wanted something that would come closer to expressing our informal way of life."

Dinah suggested that George make drawings of a few pieces of furniture. The drawings looked good, and when George came to making them out of wood, they looked even better. He made every stick of furniture in the Montgomery house.

Soon Hollywood friends began asking about the pieces, and when they learned that George had made them with his own hands, they demanded that he make them reproductions. George did so. Eventually he opened his own cabinet shop.

"I found that this hobby of mine became a profitable business—as well as a source of relaxation and pleasure—and in no way interfered with my career in pictures," he said later.

"He's the kind of guy who can make a slouch of Robinson Crusoe," Dinah marveled to friends.

She was a one hundred percent show business person during the day, but a one hundred percent housewife at night. When friends telephoned the house, asking for Miss Shore, the servants hung up, as they had been instructed.

"I'll only answer the phone if the caller asks for *Mrs. Montgomery*," Dinah told them.

Some of her friends in sophisticated Hollywood circles were amused that she should be so dead set against letting her career interfere with her marriage, but it was no joke to Dinah.

Her home life was entirely separate from her public

life. It was as if a curtain went down the moment she left the radio or recording studio and entered her home.

She had plenty of hobbies to take up her time. She loved to play tennis, to swim, and to play golf. And, although she never had a painting lesson in her life, she painted colorful roses, birds, and flowers on old-fashioned clocks. She learned how to work in oils, and turned into a rather skilled amateur painter.

Also, she continued her old hobby of photography. A young photographer, shooting her and her husband at home one day, knocked over his camera and broke it. To avoid another appointment, Dinah took him to her hobby room and asked if he could use anything she had.

"Anything" was quite a bit: A Rolleiflex, Speed Graphic, an 8 × 10 view camera, a Leica, and nearly every piece of equipment Eastman Kodak ever made.

But her main love was the kitchen.

She had always loved to cook, even as a girl in Nashville. Although the Montgomerys had a cook to do the work, Dinah always supervised.

And on Sundays, the maid's day off, she loved to spend time in the kitchen preparing Southern dishes— turnip greens and cornbread, hot-water hoe cakes, black-eyed peas, pecan pie, hominy grits, hush puppies.

"The world ought to have hominy grits for breakfast instead of fried potatoes," she once told a celebrated gourmet she happened to be breakfasting with in a posh Manhattan restaurant. He immediately turned green but recovered in time to enjoy the steak tartare that was on its way.

Hush puppies, for the uninitiated, are corn cakes garnished with onions and fried in deep fat, usually in the leavings from a fish fry.

"They get their name from the Southern hunters' custom of throwing bread scraps to their hungry, howling dogs, and crying out, 'Hush, puppies!' " At least, that was the way Dinah learned it.

Cooking was a pleasure for Dinah, but not always

for George. He once complained: "You should see how she cooks! It's like a cyclone hit. It takes her four pans to scramble a couple of eggs. They taste good, though."

He never said how many pans it took her to get her hot-water hoe cakes off the ground.

Dinah tended to be pretty informal about picking up her garments once she had cast them off, according to her meticulous and neat husband. "Also," George said once, "I wish she was a little more accurate about taking down telephone calls for me—and a little less sentimental about birthdays and holidays."

What husband hasn't said that at one time or another?

Nevertheless, George was the "perfect husband," if there ever was such a thing. He coulld make home repairs almost blindfolded. If the clothes washer went on the fritz, George got out a wrench and had it fixed in no time. If there was a leaky window, George had it caulked instantly.

The Montgomerys never went the typical Holly-wood social route—promotional events, nightclub crawling, late night snacks at famous restaurants. Nor did they go out to the social parties that everyone else did. In fact, neither one of them smoked or drank. That was enough to set them apart and build a fence around them. They went to bed early and got up early.

Their idea of a good time was to have a small bar-becue party beside the pool and to entertain their guests and themselves with good conversation and music. "Some of the Hollywood crowd may find it dull," Dinah said, "but we like it."

Because their life style was so completely out of character for Hollywood, it immediately became a legend in the press. Theirs was almost instantly dubbed "the perfect marriage" and was reported as such as many times that it became a cliché.

An interviewer once told Dinah she thought the "perfect marriage" image was all a sham. Every time she opened up a newspaper, she said, she saw photographs of Dinah and George Montgomery out at a night club or in a big posh restaurant like the Brown Derby or Chasen's. How could they be at home all that time when they were photographed so often in expensive restaurants?

Dinah laughed. "Oh, I didn't ever go out as much as that. You only go out once, they take five hundred pictures in one evening, and keep using them and it looks like you're on the town every night!"

But she admitted that beneath the image she presented of the calm and pleasant girl, she did get upset and she did have problems keeping her anger bottled up. And she definitely did keep her hurts, disappointments, and tensions to herself.

"Mother," she recalled, "had a couple of wonderful sayings: 'You don't wash your linen in public,' and 'a girl's reputation is like a white dress.' I was taught not to burden other people unduly with my problems, unless they were vitally interested."

Her philosophy of life was that she should never burden others and make them unhappy by what was upsetting her.

"Of course," she admitted, "you can take that to extremes, as I have in my lifetime, to the point where you carry everhthing yourself. Thank God for George and my sister and my brother-in-law."

It was a rare Sunday, when the Montgomerys were not at the Seligman place, or the Seligmans were not at the Montgomery's place. Dr. Seligman had become a well-known specialist in Los Angeles.

The two families loved to play tennis together, talk to each other, or just sit around reading and relaxing. Their only bone of contention was the Bessie and Dinah could never agree on the proper recipe for chili. Dinah's chili had onions in it, and Bessie's left them out.

The Seligmans were very close to Dinah and George, and helped them face their problems. "Trouble is part of your life," Dinah said, "and if you don't share it, you don't give the person who likes or loves you a chance to love you enough."

She depended a great deal on her husband to keep her from burning herself out, going off in too many different directions at once.

"George has his feet on the ground, and when I'm running over with ideas, I tell them to him. He'll say, 'I like that, that's good, but that one, now maybe . . .' He's very sensible and sees to it that I don't get carried away by my enthusiasm."

One thing she took along into her marriage from her career was her amazing ability to snatch catnaps when she was tired. Whenever, she got forty minutes to change costume and makeup, she would spend ten or fifteen minutes sleeping soundly.

And, no matter how much the pressure, she made it a point not to let anything interfere with her eating. Ordinarily, Dinah Shore ate like a gourmet truck driver, consuming four meals a day. It never affected her weight, though, because her active life and the tension to which she was exposed always burned it right off.

The Montgomery marriage was no different from other marriages. Along with the surface image of happiness and gaiety, there were certain conflicts of temperament.

Dinah, who had always had money in hand during the worst years of the Depression, and who had never been able to live within her allowance, continued her open-handed way of spending money once she was married. Why not? She had plenty. So did George.

But George, who had been brought up stringently through the Depression, had an astute sense of business and money matters. In fact, even as money piled up in the bank for him and his wife, he got tigher and stingier.

"He behaved as though every tomorrow might be a bank holiday," one observer said.

George supervised all the household expenses, from

food for the kitchen to Dinah's department-store purchases. On more than one occasion he threatened to return them all because of her carefree attitude toward the family budget.

He even refused to buy a washing machine at one time to do the family clothes. The punch line of the anecdote was his statement to the Montgomery housekeeper: "If my mother could do the laundry by hand, so can you!" Her answer, unfortunately, was never recorded.

But not even close friends ever accused George of trading on Dinah's fame. It was his business sense that was potentially responsible for their multimillion-dollar worth in community property. His motion-picture work and his custom furniture factory always earned him excellent money.

In most areas, though, the two of them shared interests and excitements. They both loved tennis and swimming. They were year-round tennis players, a perfectly matched team.

"Your true personality comes out in tennis," George once said. "With most women you have to cover more than half of the court. Not with Dinah. She plays like a man. Tenacity is the best part of her game. She has a fantastic desire to win, yet she is a gracious loser and you love her for both qualities."

Dinah enjoyed the life style in California. She liked its informal ambience and its sunshine. "In New York, you stay up too late," she said. "I had terrible insomnia. Here in California, seems like everything goes on in the daytime—you do all your worrying in the daytime. I sleep like a ton of bricks now."

And she could wear casual clothes most of the time when she wasn't appearing in front of large groups of people. She had a special rehearsal music room right in her home where she worked on her songs.

Immediately after, she could go outside and putter around in the garden for a time. Working professionally at home also meant no shoes, a state which she loved. She made a habit of kicking them off the minute she got in the house.

She once said, "As a matter of fact, I record and broadcast better with shoes off, feet planted wide apart, and hands clasped behind my back.

"When I sing," she explained, "I concentrate so thoroughly I often don't know where I am. Losing myself is important, but you pay a price. I know that because my friends tell me my posture is awful, I have my eyes shut and I make all kinds of faces.

"I've tried to correct it, but I can't. I've got to concentrate on the lyric—whatever I'm talking about in the song—and the pitch and the intonation, and the phrasing. I just can't bother how I look—whatever is my worst angle in the whole world, I suppose that's the one I give the audience." It didn't hurt her musical image any—especially on radio or records.

Dinah took some time off at the end of 1947, and on January 4, 1948, Melissa Ann Montgomery was born. The arrival of Dinah's daughter changed the whole household completely. Everything now centered around "Missy," as she came to be called.

"I really didn't want to work after Missy was born," Dinah confessed. "But George encouraged me. And of course, so did everybody else. I cut down a little bit on my radio and record work, but not really all that much." She also said that her life had become quite a bit more organized.

"Before I met George," she explained, "my life was an omelet: everything was mixed up from day to day; nothing was planned. I used to go around in sloppy sweaters, droopy skirts, and scuffed shoes. But after I was married—and the children arrived—I began to see that I couldn't live from one second to the next and be happy."

In 1949, when Missy was only one year old, Dinah took time off from her commitments on the Coast and went to New York to appear at the Waldorf-Astoria's Wedgwood Room.

The New Yorker covered the opening. In its slightly bored, raised-eyebrow style, it gently demolished her. She had done the unpardonable in the distinguished circles of the cognoscenti: she had gone to Hollywood and made a lot of money.

"After eight years away from the place," the piece began, "Dinah Shore returned to the scene of her supper-club debut, the Wedgwood Room of the Waldorf. During those eight years, the American public has become familiar with her singing style, acquired a taste for it, and perhaps, of late, grown a trifle tired of it.

"I draw this crude graph only because I think the passage of time and all those Dinah Shore records has altered one's perceptiveness to what is, at best, a slim talent for putting over a song.

"At any rate, my preconceptiveness has been altered. I caught her act the other night, and I found her singing a bit monotonous. Too much Dinah Shore over the years—I guess that's the trouble.

"Her inexperience in nightclubs lessens her appeal, too; she has confidence and is agreeable to look upon but, except for occasional awkward queries as to what the spectators would like to hear next, she is studied and aloof.

"Consequently, she invites judgment of her voice alone, and since her voice is unremarkable, her performance is, too. . . . Her orchestral accompaniments are rich-sounding and she had, in addition to her own piano player, a special conductor, Harry Zimmerman, who, by the way, leads the orchestra for her recordings.

"Miss Shore obviously comes well equipped for her club date. She has a smart new haircut, and the dress I saw her in was demure and beautiful. It's the same voice, though—nice enough in its way."

The New Yorker's "D.W." was not the only one at the Wedgwood Room to see her. Newsman Malcolm

Johnson, whose series on crime later was developed into
the hit motion picture *On the Waterfront*, also covered
her act. It was almost as if he had seen someone else,
and not the Dinah Shore *The New Yorker* man wrote
about.

"Miss Shore," he said, "is one of the first young
singers to emerge from the swing background of the last
six or seven years, and is thus truly orientated to that
way of performance . . . She sings a ballad with rhythm
and a rhythmic song with a sound sense of melodic con-
tour. In the words of Ira Gershwin, 'Who could ask for
anything more?' "

He went on: "Miss Shore is extremely attractive to
the eye, a fact that isn't exactly going to hurt her
career." In addition, he noted, "She appears to have a
supper club following."

Summing it all up, "An attractive note in the
current success is the ease with which she has made the
transition from radio and theater to the exacting demands of a hotel room. Without depending on routine
tricks, Miss Shore has created a definite personality for
herself on a floor in front of an orchestra, in which her
sincerity is a very considerable factor.

"When she sings 'Everything I Love,' or 'Blues in
the Night,' or 'Embraceable You,' or even the saucy 'I
Said No,' she just sings it the best way she knows
how—which happens to be downright insinuating and
fairly irresistible."

She wasn't really looking for a new career in the
nightclub or hotel grill circuit. She was sharpening up
her performance for something that was brand
new—something she and Ticker Freeman had been
discussing quietly for some time.

A new career?

Perhaps.

The networks had a bright and shiny toy, and really
didn't know how to play with it. Milton Berle had
plunged in, and he looked like exactly what he was: a

vaudeville comedian who now appeared on the little talking box in the bar.

Video, as it was called, was just beginning. One out of a hundred people had a set. Electronics whizzes built their own and had the neighbors in. Every corner bar had a set, which showed the wrestling matches, or the bicycle races, or the baseball games to the drinkers who crowded around.

Hollywood wanted to ignore "the box." The studio executives pretended it didn't exist. Only a handful of them let their performers appear on it.

Finally NBC allocated a large amount of "seed money" to top comic Ed Wynn, telling him to go ahead and put on one show a week with the best talent he could get.

Wynn looked on television as some fly-by-night thing that would vanish quickly. But he was game. He and a group of harried writers—most of them from radio-sat around week after week trying to concoct exciting skits for the new medium. The only trouble was, no one knew if anyone out there was really watching. The sets were dinky, the pictures kept rolling up and down, and you could hardly see the people's outlines, much less their faces.

Writers like Hal Kanter and Leo Solomon were working up ideas for Ed Wynn. But the big problem from week to week was getting talent. Yet most of the people Wynn asked to join him did appear. He paid them out of NBC's very good money bank.

But after the first show the comic was worried. "How'd it go, guys?" he asked the writers. The writers, to save their livelihoods, told Wynn he was a smash. The telephone rang while they were sitting around and performing an autopsy on the show. Someone wanted to speak to Wynn. He took the phone and listened. He beamed, he chuckled, he cooed and smiled.

When he hung up, he turned to his producer. "That was Fanny Brice, the greatest talent on the face of the earth. She thought the show was great! That's the most perfect compliment I could get! Fanny Brice!''

When the show went on for the second week, Wynn sat around with the crew, rehashing the mistakes, and the phone rang again. It was Fanny Brice. Wynn beamed. "She thought *this* was the best I've ever done! How do you like that? The greatest comedienne in the world!"

The third show was a little better, but Wynn had begun to worry. What if Fanny Brice didn't like it? He looked glum and despondent after the show, because the phone didn't ring. "I wonder what's the matter?" he moaned, ready to quit show business. "I guess we really bombed!" Then, later, the phone rang, and it was Fanny Brice. Wynn's face was wreathed in smiles. "Better than anything she ever saw before!" he told them in ecstasy. "Guys, that's the greatest talent in the world, and she *loved* me tonight!"

The fourth show went on, and now Wynn was really worried. Not only was he unhappy with the audience reaction, which had been sluggish, but he had no idea whom he could entice into coming on the show the following week. Everybody seemed to be committed.

"Who can we get?" the producer wondered. Wynn racked his brains. He couldn't think of anybody. They had used Eddie Cantor. They had used Jack Benny. Who was there left?

The phone rang.

It was Fanny Brice. Wynn listened, and hung up, happy as a clam at high tide. "Fanny said I can't go any higher after tonight's show. There's no place to go now that we've hit the top!" His elation evaporated like a popped balloon. "But who'll we get for next week?"

Everybody in the room stared at Wynn. Was he crazy? He had just talked to the top talent in Hollywood. Kanter pointed to the telephone. "But, Ed, that's who we get! We get Fanny Brice to be on with you next week!"

Wynn's face clouded. He frowned. "Fanny Brice?" he snorted. "What the hell can *she* do?"

It was about this time that a young singer from radio decided to take the plunge. And Dinah Shore was the next one on the Ed Wynn show.

Kanter and Solomon dreamed up her entry, which was, actually, her entry into television.

"It was a showboat set," Kanter reminisced, "with people entering and going up the gangplank. Ed came in and asked the ticket-taker if dinner was being served on board. 'No,' said that chap, 'if you wish to eat, you must dine ashore.'

"Dine ashore?" screamed Ed. *'Dinah Shore?'*

"And on she came," laughed Kanter. "Which is what, in those days, we called a *real entrance*."

That was her first time on television, and she never once looked back on motion pictures or on radio.

It was a major turning point in her life.

7

"See
the
U.S.A. ..."

Several lines of development that had been progressing quite independently of one another were about to come together to catapult Dinah Shore into a national fame that would give her more clout than any of her fellow singers.

Her early vocal style had been developed by hard work and analysis; usually in the form of listening to playbacks of her songs. She had started the tedious work of improving herself vocally back in Nashville, and had continued during her New York stint. Once she was established in radio, she still listened to herself, changing what she considered ineffective and constantly polishing her sound image. A recording had to be perfect before she would allow it to be released.

She had polished up her low-voiced, intimate,
bluesy style of singing a modern ballad so that each
record buyer, juke box fan, and radio listener felt she
was singing directly to him or to her. She had created a
binding communication between singer and listener
through intimate vocal technique.

Even at the peak of her radio career, she continued
to polish up her singing style by appearing frequently in
initimate settings like the Wedgwood Room of the
Waldorf Astoria.

Motion pictures had added another dimension to
her image. However, motion pictures seemed to put
distance between her and her audience. Although
movies were more intimate than stage productions,
nevertheless the big screen was set up a long way off
from the viewers. And the viewers were actually
"theater-goers," since they had to travel from their
homes to be in the movie theater.

She had never felt comfortable performing in
motion pictures; she had always preferred radio and
recording studios. Mistakenly, she thought it was
because she was not photogenic. She *was* photogenic,
but she was not really being photographed in quite the
proper fashion.

The appearance of her face on the big screen had
always bothered her. So embarrassed about her looks
was she that four years had elapsed between the production of *Belle of the Yukon* and *Aaron Slick from
Punkin' Crick*. When she agreed to make the latter she
pleaded with studio executives for help. Charles Lang, a
veteran cinematographer, went to work with the
makeup gang to try to atone for the wrongs the camera
had done her in the past.

"I couldn't understand it," Lang said. "I screened
her pictures one by one. She was really stacked, with
firm round curves. When they shot *Belle of the Yukon*
she was the only one they could put into those gay
nineties hour-glass dresses without padding out the

bosom. She had shapely legs, and yet she came over on camera like a klutz!"

Lang experimented with various makeups and lighting placements, and finally hit upon a combination that actually featured the interesting facial planes in Dinah's face that had been wiped out or fuzzed by shadows before. In fact, in several of the shots in that movie, she looked fresh and appealing for the first time.

The problem with *Aaron Slick* wasn't Dinah's looks; it was the story and the treatment that had ruined it.

When television appeared on the scene, it was the obvious thing for the pundits to nod wisely and say that the new medium combined both radio and motion pictures. However, many of the early television producers overlooked one important difference. Television was an *initmate* medium, not a big-screen medium. In fact, the big movie spectaculars tended to become diminished when they were shown over television.

Early TV shows resembled one-act dramas, performed as a stage play would be performed. Outdoor action shows were filmed exactly as motion pictures were—panoramas, long shots, crowd scenes. And, as such, they looked all wrong on the tiny screen.

In the early days, television was an oddity that seemed to collect people in front of it. It was, in effect, a movie screen in miniature. In the bars, scores of people would watch over their beers. In restaurants during World Series time, crowds of diners would watch over their Reuben sandwiches. At first, television owners would invite neighbors in from up and down the street to see Uncle Miltie or the bike races.

But not for long. The gadget-happy American people were always ready for a new fad. Soon there were sets in a large percentage of homes. And quickly television became what it was intended to be: *intimate*, instant communication.

It was the perfect medium for Dinah, who had not

consciously modeled herself for it, but who was a natural to exploit it and make the most of it. As she sang directly to the mike in a studio, so she sang and spoke directly to the television viewer.

Her ability to project her personality instantly to the viewer made her seem to be right there in the viewer's own home.

Once she found out how powerfully she affected the viewers, she capitalized on her own instinct for warm, human communication. Never had she forgotten Eddie Cantor's warning about coming on too strong. She relaxed, she sang, and she talked intimately to the person out there.

No one had ever done it better. No one, in fact, had even *tried* to do it the way she dared. But that's getting ahead of the story.

For months complicated talk sessions went on behind the scenes. The Chevrolet Division of General Motors made no secret of it: they wanted to sell cars not only to men but to women as well. Dinah Shore had already proved herself as a "seller" with the servicemen in World War II. Her image was that of the girl next door, she was no sex pot. The women, it was hoped, would approve of having her in *their* homes.

The idea was to come up with a show that would be melodic, tasteful, and eye-catching. For such a format, without any other continuity except the songs, the show's executives decreed that it should run for only fifteen minutes but should appear two nights a week, Tuesdays and Thursdays.

Dinah and Ticker met with Henry Jaffe, her financial advisor, and found themselves a producer and writer in Alan Handley, an ex-actor who had at one time been almost everything else as well—an architect, an author of a whodunit titled *Kiss Your Elbow*, and a manager for Jinx and Tex McCrary.

The style of the show was to be one of relaxed informality, as if the show were happening spontaneously in someone's living room. It was to be low-keyed, so as not to intrude upon the people watching, but to be part of their quiet evening at home.

Handley's job was to give each song a visual showcase so that it would play to the eye as well as to the ear. In the words of the NBC brass: "Get a pretty background for a girl singer."

Whatever Handley did, it seemed to work. The show bowed in the first week of December, 1951.

Dinah was ready, and so were the technicians who put on her makeup and photographed her. Suddenly—although it was not really all that sudden—she appeared as a beautiful, poised woman with fine, soft lines in her face and body and a golden exuberance that was pleasant and eye-arresting.

Actually, she didn't rocket to the moon like the astronauts. She started out in the twice-a-week fifteen-minute spot just like anyone else, and slowly began amassing viewers week after week.

Variety liked the show from the start. Criticizing it from a professional point of view, it gave credit for its slickness to Alan Handley. "Handley's best idea, in fact, was to give Miss Shore full rein, with a minimum of distracting background 'business.' Miss Shore carries off the assignment with a charm and ease that established her right off as one of video's standout personalities."

John Crosby, one of the toughest and most astute radio-television critics of the time, and the darling of the sophisticates and intellectuals, was quite taken with the show too.

"Hers is a very personal voice," he wrote. "One that on records or on radio or TV seems directed at you, exclusive of all others, a great trick if you can do it."

He also wrote: "*The Dinah Shore Show* is a triumph of simplicity and because it is so simple, obviously, a good deal of hard, constructive thoughts has gone into it.''

After commenting on the moves of the camera, the skits having to do with Dinah's personal life story, and her songs, he went on, ''She is the Joe DiMaggio of singers, a complete switch hitter who can tackle any sort of song—though ballads are her dish of tea.'' He mentioned the ''haunting, lilting quality, that no one else has succeeded in imitating.'' He praised her showmanship, pointing out that the selection of songs, their arrangements, the phrasing, and the whole bag of vocal tricks that went into each one of them had got better since she started in show business in 1938.

''No small credit should go to Ticker Freeman, who has been with her since her start in 1938, and who contributed nightly to the direction of the show.''

Crosby wrote that Dinah's genius was that she seemed to be speaking to each person out there watching and saying: ''Come on over here. I want to show you something.'' She was, he said, ''*the* intimate personality for the intimate medium.''

On the first night, quite by accident, Dinah came up with a ''gimmick'' that became the trademark of the show. The first fifteen-minute program went off without a hitch, and, in fact, moved so fast that the final number wound down thirty seconds before time to cut.

''Go out there and stretch it,'' Handley hissed in her ear.

''What'll I do?'' Dinah whispered back, panicky at the thought of standing there like an idiot and grinning emptily at the audience.

'''Throw them a kiss, or something,'' he said, right off the top of his head.

Dinah got out in front of the camera and smiled at the audience, mugging just a bit, letting the applause sound, trying to let the clapping carry her through. But then, unhappily, the clapping died down and there was almost dead silence, as if they were all waiting for her to say something.

So she did just what Handley, in desperation, had suggested. She put her hand to her mouth in a corny, exaggerated gesture, kissed her fingers, and blew the kiss out at the world with a very loud "ummm-wah!"

Then she ran off and the show was over.

The second show wound up, time-wise, right on the nose. Dinah finished her number and vanished.

Letters poured in by the bundles. "What? No good night kiss? How can I sleep tonight?" And so on.

Needless to say, on the *third* show, the kiss was written in and delivered in the same manner it had been the first night. The kiss became the trade mark of Chevvy, Dinah Shore, and nighttime television.

The final arbiter of taste and talent on the show was always Dinah.

Working with Ticker Freeman to select, arrange, and prepare the songs on the show, she knew exactly what she was doing and why. It was no accident that she was soon to become the number-one personality on television. Her accurate and concise analysis of television singing and of its difference from radio singing told the whole story.

"For radio and phonograph records, a song doesn't have to make much sense—the audience is listening mostly to the melody—but in television the lyrics have to make sense or you can't communicate with the audience," she said. "You have the audience's full attention and you have to say something, not just a bunch of words."

For radio and recording, she explained, the singer could vary his or her position to the microphone, moving in close or away from it to create different effects. In television, with the microphone usually placed over the head of the singer, this tonal quality had to be sacrificed for a more effective "visual" singing of the lyrics.

"The warmth and feeling and personality that a singer puts into the words of a song more than compensates for the loss in technical quality of the music," she felt. She tried to phrase the lyrics in a convincing and natural style, expressing the *mood* of the lyric. "I try to believe what I'm saying," she observed, "in much the same way that an actress *feels* a part."

She knew her way with the written material, too. She tended to play the skits in the spirit they were written—as fill-in material to be mugged through rather than "acted." Dinah didn't like to act. She "faked." "I'm a pretty good faker—out of necessity," she said. No actor, she mugged; no dancer, she pretended so well that she often made the pros on the stage with her look as if they were on the wrong foot.

"I'm not intimidated by pressure or competition," Dinah noted. "Television is a live, responsive medium with personal contact and pressure. I respond to it. I guess it's the hambone in me."

She preferred live television to motion picture work or filmed television for the same reason that she consistently scheduled appearances at nightclubs and cocktail lounges.

It was the spontaneity of it, the *reality*. Live television and a live audience were a lot more exciting to her than filmed television with its amplified laugh track.

"A TV program is clocked with stop watches," she explained. "Every number in it is carefully rehearsed. What happens between numbers is rehearsed too. Even audience reaction is controlled. If audible approval is desired, lights go up behind an APPLAUSE sign. But, no matter how rigidly you channel it, there's a human equation in live TV that gives it spur-of-the-moment touches."

In one of the early shows, Dinah was singing "Red

Sails in the Sunset." The script called for her to step off a gondola and wave goodbye to it as it sailed off down a Venetian Canal. Unfortunately, the gondola had got beached somehow. It *didn't* sail away. It just sat there on the stage like a big dead lump. One dancer walked through the water and pushed it away as Dinah continued singing, trying to keep the laughter out of her voice.

"Anything can happen," she said. "You can make capital of a bad moment by laughing at it instead of treating it as if it were the end of the world. Handled right, a booboo adds spontaneity. It can give you a feeling of kinship with viewers that's a big, fat plus."

Contrary to rumors, none of the booboos on the show were written into the script. They really happened accidentally. Because of their success at establishing an informal atmosphere, other imitative shows began writing in fluffs and errors, just for the laughs.

There were moments that were scary, too. During one program Dinah was plagued by an inability to remember the lines of a certain song she was scheduled to sing. The action in the skit took place on a street in the Casbah at Algiers. Dinah was to walk down the street, singing several songs, while snake charmers played flutes and beggers beseeched alms from her.

By show time, she still had not mastered the third of the three numbers she was to sing. For some reason she had a mental block against it. Ticker Freeman asked her if she wanted a cue card set up so she could refresh her memory. She refused, determined to remember the words *without* the idiot card.

The show started. She sang her first song while she mulled over postcards at a bazaar on the street. She sang song number two seated at a sidewalk café. The third number was the one she had been having trouble with. During the commercial break, Ticker came over to her and whispered the words into her ear. She nodded, sure she would remember. Then she walked on camera as the introduction began on cue.

Her mind went absolutely blank. She could not remember the words at all. But the irrepressible Ticker had prepared cue cards in spite of her orders not to. Dinah breathed a sigh of relief as she saw him put up the first card. Then she looked closer, blinked, and started to laugh.

He had written the card in fake Arabic lettering—not English! She couldn't read a word.

Dinah was laughing hard now. And all the tension drained out of her. Relaxed, she remembered the words and went on to sing the song, laughing all the way through it.

Ticker's gag had released her from the psychological impasse she had experienced. The audience remembered how she had been so amused at the song she was singing—but nobody outside the show knew why.

It was a fun show to watch because anything could happen—and usually did.

The whole show was in her control, and her decisions were final. She was not consistently right—no one ever has been—and when anyone critized her, she was not happy about accepting disparaging remarks. Yet she tended to listen to her associates.

Once her press agent knocked one show, and then retired moodily to the hospital with an ulcer attack, quite certain that he would be terminated for his blunt critique. However, after he returned, Dinah invited him to sit in on future postmortems.

In the highly competitive show business atmosphere of television, Dinah was admired for the calm and pleasant way in which she operated.

"She appears casual on television only because she's a perfectionist and knows what she's doing," one of her producers, Bob Banner, said. "People on the show are interested in working as hard as she does. I don't have to push them. It's contagious."

She constantly tried innovations and worked to freshen up old formulas. Although warm and friendly, she demanded and got the best from others, as she demanded and got the best from herself.

"If you deliver," an associate said, "she is eternally grateful. If you say, 'This is the best we can do, given this time and money,' you won't last out the season."

Dinah knew herself very well. "It drives people crazy. But I'm never *quite* satisfied. You know, there are always things you're not ecstatic about."

An associate put it another way. "She lives life as if she doesn't want to miss anything."

On the other side of the coin, she unnerved her sponsors by her lackadaisical manner of arriving at departure time for long trips. She would never appear more than minutes before the deadline. Once she dashed into an airport fifty seconds before takeoff, trailed by twenty-two suitcases and a retinue of perspiring servants.

"Being Dinah," a friend observed, "she probably could have spread her arms and taken off by herself." The record shows, however, that she did not, and that the jet plane took her where she was scheduled to go.

She did have her impulsive moments relative to travel. Once her sister Bessie was driving her down to Union Station in Los Angeles where she was slated to board the eastbound train. "Gee, it's a nice day," she said to her sister. "Why don't we *drive* by to New York?"

Bessie turned to her, stared, giggled, and said, "Why not?"

And they did.

"We had us a ball," Dinah reported weeks later when they finally returned to Los Angeles with a whole new wardrobe of clothes.

"*The Dinah Shore Show*" made its hostess a

household word within the first few years of its ten-year life. In fact, she was an almost instant success. Television had the ability to make instant stars, instant personalities, instant politicans. She was one.

She was watched by everyone. "One of the smoothest performers in show business," a critic wrote, "Dinah is liked equally by teenagers, housewives, and all-male audiences."

Her guests ranged from well-established stars of stage, screen, and radio to those who had never before been seen by American audiences. She became the female Eddie Cantor of her time, introducing to the television world such luminaries as Maureen O'Hara, Gene Barry, Craig Stevens, Yves Montand, Stephen Boyd, Ingemar Johansson, and Rossano Brazzi—to name only a handful.

"I think people come off well on the show, and they're happy about it," Dinah said. "We have never had any disgruntled guests that I know of. We work hard, but we enjoy it. And very often, we stay friends forever after."

The backgrounds for her songs ranged from up-side-down sets and double images of Dinah, to sets containing Alexander Calder's mobiles, and all the way to skits with a singing quintet forming a living mobile swinging from the ceiling.

"She is one of those rare persons capable of coming through the tube at you," said Handley. "She generates energy on TV which wouldn't come through in movies because the continuity is broken so often."

She had her own ideas of why she was a success. It was her aim, she told an admirer, to produce "a light, dependable program ever in good taste and with a high degree of professionalism."

And she did it.

The Chevrolet brass were ecstatic. For ten years, right up into the fall of 1961, when she began a reduced schedule, Chevvy sponsored her and listened to the jangle of cash registers as Americans bought Chevrolets by the millions to the tune of Dinah's voice singing "See the U.S.A in Your Chevrolet . . ."

And she was *busy* even off the show.

In 1957, just for example, she made a ten-thousand-mile tour of the country for the American Heart Association and other charities, making personal appearances, addressing a State Legislature, and singing for the Shriners' luncheon and with the Philadelphia Symphony. Then she worked three weeks in Las Vegas at a nightclub.

It was not all peaches and cream in her home life. Her skyrocketing fame was taking its toll on her family life. She and her husband still make it a habit not to nightclub about or go to Hollywood parties. In fact, she was absolutely adamant against doing anything that might interfere with time spent with her family.

But there was no doubt about it, the Montgomerys were very busy people. George's schedule of making motion pictures and managing his furniture company kept him running at as fast a pace as his wife's.

But come hell, high water, motion pictures, or command performances, they met for a six-thirty dinner with their daughter, Melissa Ann.

When Melissa was just beginning to talk, Dinah used to sing to her in the car. But soon that brought an unusual reaction from the little girl. One day she put her finger across Dinah's lips. "Tell me a thtory, Mommy," she lisped. "Don't thing!"

It was a shattering thing for Dinah to realize her daughter didn't like to her her sing. The whole country did—why not Melissa?

It was Dinah's sister Bessie who straightened Dinah out, acting as a family psychiatric consultant practicing without a license: "Don't you see? Melissa associates your singing with going to the studio and leaving her!"

Dinah saw the point of that. And it brought about a change in the Montgomerys' life style.

Finally Dinah talked George into moving from their Encino home to Beverly Hills, where she would be only fifteen minutes from NBC's Hollywood studios. In the morning Dinah drove Melissa to school and then went to the studio.

One evening when Dinah came home and was playing with Melissa just before supper, she saw that her daughter was staring at her in a rather surprised, questioning way.

"What is it, Missy?"

"I know who you are," Missy said in a low, accusing voice.

"Then, who am I?" Dinah asked, thinking it was a game.

"You're Dinah Shore."

"Dinah blinked. "Of course I'm Dinah Shore."

Melissa turned away from her, wouldn't have anything to do with her.

Dinah finally saw the point of her daughter's resistance. "Dinah Shore" was *somebody else*—somebody out of the house, on the television set, at the studio, Mrs. George Montgomery was Melissa's mother. Dinah Shore was an outsider.

"But I'm your mother, too," Dinah finally told her.

"As long as you're not Dinah Shore," said Melissa, and turned to her and kissed her and made up.

In the early 1950's Melissa was becoming moodier and moodier. One day Dinah watched her as Melissa sat at the window looking out into the bright warm sunlight where the neighborhood children were at play.

"Melissa Ann Montgomery," Dinah said, "a penny for your thoughts!"

"I just wish that I had a hundred brothers and sisters!" she responded instantly.

That made Dinah think about a problem she had not really allowed herself to face. After her daughter's birth, she had had no other children.

"There was no reason why," she said, "at least none the doctors could discover. And when that's the case, it's hard to make up your mind about adoption. But I realized at that moment that there had been too much waiting, too much hoping and too much mental postponing." She decided that she must consult with her husband.

"I don't want Melissa raised as an only child," she told him. "She's a happy little girl, but she's alone, and that's not too good for any youngster. We've given her too much love. I think she'd like to share it with a brother or sister."

George didn't think too much of the idea of adoption. It seemed uncalled-for. "People don't adopt babies in Montana, Dinah," he told her. "They *have* them."

Dinah didn't argue. It was against her nature. However, the Montgomerys simply weren't *having* them. She brought up the subject again. She pointed out to her husband what a lonely life she had had—with her sister Bessie eight years older than she, and no companionship at all for her. George, who had grown up in a crowded environment, one of fifteen kids, finally got the message.

They filed for adoption. And waited. The wait strung on and on, seemingly forever, but it was actually less than two years when they were called to meet their new son, whom they immediately named John David. As he grew up, he became known as "Jody."

Jody was a delight to Dinah and George from the beginning, but not so to Melissa. As was common in such a situation, she became increasingly jealous. Even though every effort was made to include her in the joy of romping with the new baby, she would go off and do something naughty to attract attention. Sometimes she kicked the servants in the shins and invented other ingenious torments for members of the household.

Then, when she was reprimanded, she would run to her father for comfort.

"After a series of particularly annoying clashes with Melissa," a servant related, "I spanked her and was told rather sternly that the children were *not* to be punished. Mrs. Montgomery seemed to feel that if her children were loved enough, they would always behave."

One day Melissa approached her mother with a sad face, and said:

"Mommy, you *picked* Jody didn't you? But you were kind of stuck with me, weren't you?"

Dinah was flabbergasted at the depressing thought expressed, and hastened to explain to Melissa that she was not "stuck" at all with Melissa, and that there was love enough in the family for both Melissa and her brother.

About that time Melissa became quite taken with the story of Cinderella. She loved the pumpkin carriage and the nice footmen. And she loved Cinderella, who had so much trouble with her ugly stepmother and her stepsisters, but who won the prince anyway.

One night she gave her mother a big hug.

"What's that for?" Dinah asked in pleased surprise.

"On account of you're such a nice mummy. I just love you."

"That's good," Dinah said. "I'm delighted to hear it."

"I only hope," Melissa said, thinking of Cinderella, "I'm going to love my stepmother as much."

Dinah stared at her a moment in shock, then recovered gallantly. "Don't worry about it. I'm terribly healthy."

Even though she was busy, Dinah found time to fool around with photography and to dabble in oil painting. And once she got going on her painting, she developed a facility working in a primitive style.

"If I'm not careful," George said, "I'll wind up married to Grandma Moses."

More than one awed interviewer asked her how she managed to combine career and marriage.

"I do have a full schedule," she admitted, "but it doesn't interfere with my family life. Missy, George, Jody, and I breakfast together. I don't leave home until Missy's gone to school. And I have time to play with my youngest, Jody, in the morning."

She then planned the menus and helped sort out the day for the household, she said. Once that was in hand, she started out for the television studio. Returning home abour four-thirty, she had more time with the children.

"If I get home later than four-thirty, Missy will have had her bath, and will have done some of her homework. Then we can have our afternoon coffee together." Dinah laughed. "Coffee at the Montgomerys isn't really *coffee* at all. It's cocoa or ginger ale for Missy and Jody. And George and I have tea."

"I combine career and marriage by working hard at it," she told a writer. "What most people take for granted is what I have to work the hardest for. My family means more to me than anything in the world—nothing will ever interfere with that."

She explained how she and her husband managed to get along together as well. "We respect each other's work and never interfere unless we are asked for advice."

Her philosophy of life had a lot to do with her ability to rise above problems, she said. "I live in the present. I forget everything that happened yesterday. Every morning when I get up, I know it's going to be the best day I've ever spent."

Dinah Shore saw herself as a total optimist.

"I've always been a 'today' person," she said. "It would be interesting to have a psychologist explain it to me, but I wouldn't really have the time to listen."

She also believed that everything that ever happened to her—even the bad things—happened for a reason.

"In my case, they've resulted in my going in a direction that's better for me. My misadventures with the movies are a case in point. If I had made out in motion pictures my life would have been entirely different. I'm so glad I didn't, I could bust."

Television, she said, was a great boon to the mothers who worked in it.

"When I made my last picture I saw very little of my family. Besides, I was so keyed up from working all day that, tired as I was, I had trouble falling asleep. That was my idyllic life as a motion picture actress. You can have it."

Dinah knew that her career and her life style were potential dangers to the happiness of her children. "This is a funny town we're raising our children in," she said. "They're going to need every bit of the strength of personality and character we can give them later on in life.

"Both George and I are positive and strong. Sometimes it's not easy to be, but I think it's important."

Optimism, confidence, love—those were the keystones of Dinah Shore's character. In addition, she sometimes relied on a power greater than herself, a power that manifested itself in odd ways.

It was the old extrasensory perception. "I don't believe that I have special powers, or anything like that," she said. "But at times, I've sensed it when one of my children needed me for something, or my sister, or even a very close friend.

"And when I called or checked, sure enough, the person would say, 'I've been trying to reach you,' or 'I was wishing you'd call.'

"I do believe that when you love someone very much, you can feel vibrations coming from them even if you are many miles apart."

Dinah's incurable optimism tended to obscure the finer, more subtle points of conflict and dissension that were making their appearance in her close family circle. It was her nature to look at the good things and never see the bad. Also, her associates tried to buoy her up, ignoring the warning signals that were flashing repeatedly, and pretending everything was coming up roses.

Although they never told her so, her co-workers and associates were quite aware that there was something going wrong in the Montgomery family.

In 1957 the twice-a-week show was changed to a one-hour weekly performance on Sunday evenings. And at that time, there was even more pressure on the family.

"When Dinah was doing the Chevvy show, the telecast went live to the East at six P.M. on Sundays," one of the show's writers said. "After the show, Dinah seldom closed shop. Instead, she often invited the staff to her home. We'd have a ball watching the nine o'clock Coast playback, then sit up until around midnight discussing next week's plans.

"If George wasn't out at their San Fernando Valley ranch with the children, he'd sit in for awhile, but he must have been pretty bored by talk about something in which he had no part. He usually retired early because he had to get up at six A.M. and ride a horse."

To most of her colleagues, Dinah Shore was not really a simple country girl at all. She was a highly intelligent sophisticate. George was not. George was intelligent, but he was too honest and straightforward to don a fake aura of sophistication.

"I'd say that George is 'Day People,' " a friend said, "while Dinah is 'Night People.' "

In fact, one of the problems was that Dinah never cared particularly for country living, while George relished everything ranchy—perferences that were actual throwbacks to their respective upbringings.

Not much of this inside story got into the newspapers or magazines. Since the beginning of the Dinah Shore television show for Chevvy, the network publicists had decided to bear down heavily on "the perfect marriage" image of the Montgomerys.

It was a natural. They truly did not smoke or drink. They did not party. They lived their own lives away from the celebrity swirl.

The resulting publicity presented some amusing contradictions. One story might say: "Since the start of her increasingly successful TV career, Dinah has emerged as a full-fledged glamour queen." Another might say: "Dinah is as homey as the shoo-fly pie she sings about!"

No matter what story appeared, it would say at one point, "Theirs is said to be one of Hollywood's happiest marriages."

Dinah herself liked to be with people. In fact, she *liked* people. She loved to hear their problems. She *empathized* with them, and liked to help them when she could.

For example, one night she was watching a television show in which a university choral group was singing. A young girl stepped forward for a solo. Somehow she started in the wrong key, and couldn't get into the right one. The number was a shambles, and the girl was obviously distraught.

Dinah was on her feet dialing the broadcasting station even before the number was over. She asked for the studio from which the girl was singing and when she was told that the girl was still on she said:

"Please give her a message for me. It's terribly important. Tell her that what just happened to her could happen to any singer and does happen to most at one time or another. It happened to me once and I thought I was going die. Tell her she has a beautiful voice and that her career should be just beginning. Tell her this is very important and wish her luck."

When she was off the phone she turned to George. "A thing like that could ruin a girl's life. I hope she's going to be all right."

"It was all a part of the real Dinah Shore. But it made her look too good to be true.

Naturally, the image makers zeroed in on the "sweetness and light" that Dinah projected when she appeared on the television screen.

One critic analyzed her charm by concluding that her greatest asset was her ability to induce the feeling of happy well-being in her audience.

But there were holdouts who failed to succumb to the Dinah charm.

Art Carney claimed that he had proof her smile was actually painted on, and could be taken off with paint remover.

Oscar Levant said, "I can't watch Dinah Shore. My doctor won't let me. I'm a diabetic."

In spite of the press and the picture of her as Little Miss Polyanna, Dinah was as human as any other performer. She had her moments of private rage when she would hurl a hairbrush across her dressing room, or slam a pair of shoes at the floor in frustration.

"I'm not a shouter," she confessed, "though I may be a sulker." She sulked particularly when people said she was a "great personality" but not much of a singer. "I'm a good singer and I work hard at it—and my feelings get hurt."

But the sulking always melted quickly away under her natural sunniness, which she attributed to her philosophy of "living today."

"Her enthusiasm is real," a coworker said. "She has never quite gotten over being that hambone cheerleader at Hume-Fogg High."

It was a good thing her enthusiasm was real. In several years she would need all of it she could muster. There would be absolutely nothing in her life to cheer about.

8

Blues
in the
Night

While Dinah Shore's career kept rising and expanding, George Montgomery's hit a plateau and then finally began to sink. By no means was he struck down and forced into premature retirement, nor was he in any way rendered penniless.

In fact, his motion pictures had always brought him a good solid income, even in the declining years of his career. Between them, he and his wife made close to a million dollars a year in the 1950's. George's contribution was around $350,000 from his motion picture commitments and his furniture factory. Being an astute financial manager, he kept a wise grip on his money and did not fritter it away.

The differences between husband and wife, which had always existed in their very natures, became gradually more pronounced. As Dinah expanded her entourage of friends and associates, George narrowed his—or so it seemed.

By the very nature of the business he was in, George was through at five o'clock. At that hour, Dinah was at the peak of her day's activities.

There was also the fact that television was expanding and growing more amd more powerful, and the motion picture business was stagnating, or, as some said, shrinking slightly. Personalities who were known as motion picture stars were gradually being wooed over to the new medium. Theater attendance plummeted while television viewing soared astronomically.

Dinah was on the ship that was headed for the moon; George was on the ship that was capsizing and in danger of sinking.

As the Chevvy show rolled onward to greater and greater acclaim and triumph, Dinah made her way repeatedly to the Gallup Poll list of the Ten Most Admired Women in the World. She garnered a mantelful of Emmy's for her work in the new medium. She had already won nineteen golden records, each record selling a million or more.

Meanwhile, George, who had started out in high-budget motion pictures, costarring with Hollywood's top talent—Ginger Rogers, Betty Grable, and others —was appearing more and more in middle- or low-budget "oaters" with unknown names and dubious scripts.

George was no macho chauvinist. But he was a masculine, thoroughly assertive person whose background had provided him with a clear picture of what marriage should be. The husband should be the breadwinner; the wife should bear and raise the children. His remark to Dinah about adoption—"In Montana we don't adopt children, we *have* them"— was typical of his attitude.

If the statement might sound crass today, it was

certainly not crass or even startling in the 1950's when it was uttered. Nor did Dinah think it crass at all. She believed as much as George believed that men and women served different and complimentary roles in a marriage. She had always considered marriage superior to a career.

"I have only one fear—that if the time comes when the public no longer demands me and being a wife becomes a full-time job, I'll not make as much a success of it as I have of the part-time one," she said. "Right now I'm a successful career woman. In ten years I'll tell you if I'm a successful woman."

It was—sadly—a prophetic statement.

The home life of the Montgomerys for many years was an extremely happy one. Only when Dinah's career outstripped George's did chinks begin to appear in the surface of "Hollywood's most successful marriage." The press agent's happy image of the pair was a definite albatross the two of them carried around day after day. In the end, it was part of the paraphernalia of public relations that doomed the marriage.

Dinah knew the dangers of overstepping the bounds of her wifely role. She did everything she could to keep from dominating George.

"Although some people who have worked with Dinah on her television shows will tell you that she is quietly domineering and runs every last detail with an iron fist in a velvet glove, this was never true so far as George was concerned," a friend of the family said.

"He is all man and has never been bossed. Dinah's constant concern about his business ventures has been voiced only in the most subtle terms."

The criticisms referred to came about as a result of George's dissatisfaction with the roles he was getting in Western pictures. He had actually not lived up to his earlier potential. He felt he was going downward, and it roiled him because at the same time his wife's potential was being realized.

One of the reasons George's Westerns weren't doing well at the box office in the 1950's was because of the success of television Westerns: *Maverick, Gunsmoke, Dodge City,* and others. It was only reasonable that he should be asked to take the plunge. He did. In 1958 he made 26-hour-long segments of a series called *Cimarron City*, in which he played the sheriff of a Western town.

NBC bankrolled the series. George touted it on his wife's show. Everybody tried to help. The series simply bombed. What killed it was its position in the time slot opposite *Gunsmoke*—the most redoubtable of all the TV Westerns.

The unhappy and rapid demise of George's one attempt to equal his wife's success in the new medium was a bad setback for the relationship between husband and wife. Since her ascendency in television, Dinah had always tried to play down her own success and build up her husband's. But it was difficult to pretend that George's failure had not happened.

"She is an impossible romantic," a friend observed, "and always has been a bad judge of character, someone who always protects the underdog and ascribes character traits to people they don't have. And she's loyal to the point of sometimes being foolish."

She was becoming desperate at this point about her marriage. For all the reams of copy attesting to theirs as a perfect union, she and her husband couldn't break down the communications barrier that seemed always to have been there between them.

Dinah's interests were broad and catholic, reaching out into areas that held no interest at all for George. Although this difference in their points of view might have been aired out and resolved, Dinah could never bring herself to a confrontation of any kind with her husband.

"The real problem was that we were too bright with each other all the time," she said. "We couldn't tell each other our troubles. The whole world had an image of us and so did we, a beautiful Technicolor image. We never quarreled; he never knew what deeply troubled me and I never knew what deeply troubled him. If you don't share your private distress and sadness there is something fundamentally wrong with the relationship. In the end, we just drifted apart.''

That inability to discuss personal problems had been deeply ingrained in her since childhood, a throwback to her deep dread at the sound of her parent's arguments.

''There's a wall around her that nobody penetrates,'' her longtime financial manager and agent, Henry Jaffe, said. ''She never shows her real feelings in public. She's easily hurt and terribly sensitive. She wants more than anything else to be loved, and I don't think I've ever seen her really show anger. I'm sorry about that. She'd probably be better off if she could blow off some steam.''

The irony of the situation was that it was not Dinah who had wanted her to continue her career after the birth of her daughter Melissa, but George.

''He had fought so hard for his career that he thought it would be foolish for me to give up mine,'' Dinah said. She admitted that she did not ever fully understand her husband, or recognize his potentialities and limitations.'' And all this time, I was creating images that weren't his fault, endowing him with qualities that he just couldn't have.''

On his side, George idolized her. ''He once told me that if he couldn't cut it with *this* lady, he'd never be able to,'' a friend said.

After the debacle of *Cimarron City,* George sought some other way to assert himself professionally. He had directed one picture earlier but it had been a Western. It was simply ''another B picture.''

Now he decided to strike out on his own and become an important person in the motion picture business. Obviously the adulation accorded the European *auteurs*—motion picture makers—who produced, wrote, and directed their own movies had struck a sensitive chord in George. If *they* could do it—so could he. Or so he hoped.

The result of his infatuation with cinema as an art form was a pair of motion pictures he produced, wrote, directed, and in addition, starred in himself.

And what was Dinah's reaction when she heard about his project?

"George has a serious fault in that he tries to do too much by himself," an observer commented. There were endless examples. Witness, for instance, his almost fanatical determination to make every stick of furniture in the Montgomery home. Witness his interest in designing and helping build several of the houses in which he and Dinah lived.

Dinah had always known about this trait of his. Now she anticipated the pitfalls her husband might encounter if he tried to make real movies himself. She tried to dissuade him from taking on all the complicated and crucial responsibilities in a many-faceted profession like motion pictures. She urged him to hire expert directors and technicians and to limit his role to starring in the movies. He could mastermind the production, but it would be an error to become a Renaissance man and try to do it all!

"Money is no problem," she told him. "You can afford experts for at least two of the chief responsibilities—the writing and the directing."

She did not press him too hard, because it was not her nature to do so. She simply suggested to him the difficulties involved in the enormously difficult task he was assuming.

However, George opted to do everything himself, in spite of her pleas.

He had always wanted to make a picture about the Philippines at the beginning of World War II. Working with Malvin Wald and Ferde Grofé Jr., the son of the composer of *The Grand Canyon Suite, Mississippi Suite*, and other symphonic tone poems, George wrote a screenplay about a group of guerrillas and their trials and tribulations during the Japanese invasion.

Then he spent three months on location in the islands, directing and acting in the picture. He sent letters regularly back to Dinah in California.

Unfortunately, the letters concerned production snags and problems of photography in the jungle. None of the letters told her how much he missed her or how much he loved her.

"Letters you receive from your husband are filled with how much he misses and loves you," Dinah confided to the wife of an associate. "All my husband ever writes about is how the picture is going."

The shooting of the picture was completed after interminable problems. It was titled *The Steel Claw*. The cast included George, Charito Luna, Mario Barri, and Paul Sorensen.

The picture was eventually edited, cut, and ready for showing. At a preview screening in Hollywood, all Dinah's friends were there to help out with the cheering.

Reported a friend: "When the picture was previewed, Dinah did her utmost to focus attention on George's achievement, even though the picture was mediocre at best."

Actually, the picture was not really mediocre. Released in the fall of 1961, it was well conceived within the parameters of the action-adventure milieu. Although Bosley Crowther gave it a lukewarm review, treating it the way he treated all action pictures. "George Montgomery plays an American Marine Captain who co-commands a group of Filipino guerrillas at the outset of World War II. In the cool of the evening, when not fighting, he lightly makes chopchop love with a Filipino girl, played by Charito Luna, and . . .

"Well, it's in color, anyway."

The picture outlasted his derisive comment, but was no blockbuster at the box office. However, later on, when it was moved over onto the television late late show schedule, it began to pick up some acclaim.

Movies on TV said: "Marine about to be discharged because of the loss of a hand organizes guerrillas when the Japanese invade the Philippines. Fine photography, plenty of action compensate for a weak script in this frequently exciting war drama, very capably directed by Montgomery."

Nevertheless, at the time of the preview, it was disappointingly apparent that the movie was not going to be another *Gone With The Wind*.

"It was a bad evening," said one of the Montgomerys' friends. "When the film was over, everyone clustered around Dinah. The sight of George, standing apart, almost alone, while Dinah tried to maneuver her way to him through a mob of chattering sycophants, illustrates to me how they were constantly being thrust apart by pressures neither of them could control."

During that preview's aftermath, George bit his lip and managed to keep up the facade of small talk—at which he was no master—and smile at all the false compliments.

It would have taken no genius to see where the clout in that group lay—it was with Dinah. No matter what he did, he would never make it among the sophisticates in her group.

Yet the very dynamics of adulation toward Dinah prodded her into trying to make George the focus of attention. It became obvious to everyone that she *wanted* the picture to be good, that she wanted the same fame for her husband as she had.

"Too much help from a wife can generate a lot of unspoken bitterness in a man," one friend observed.

It had already happened before, and it would continue to happen.

During his work in the Philippines, George had

become interested in the history of the islands. And he had pretty much decided to make another film in the same locale, using a story line developed from a historical uprising in the late eighteen-hundreds.

When the second script was finished, he announced to Dinah that he was once again heading for the jungles to make a picture. She simply told him she hoped he would succeed. Asked later by a confidante why she didn't go with him, she said, "I wasn't invited."

Samar was made the year following *The Steel Claw*. George had met Ziva Rodann, a bright young actress from Haifa, Israel, who struck him as excellent for the lead opposite him. When she said she would like to do the picture with him, he invited her to the Montgomery house to discuss the part.

There Dinah met the young actress. She told her she thought she would be perfect for the part in the picture.

"About a month later, in the fall of 1960," Ziva said, "I joined the company in Manila. There were only five Americans in the cast. We all stayed at the same hotel and naturally became close friends."

Ziva said she sensed that George was a "deeply troubled man." During the three months of filming, his communications with Dinah were almost entirely about the production aspects of the picture, rather than about each other.

"On the other hand," Ziva said, "George spoke frequently in loving terms about his children, whom he sometimes called by long-distance telephone."

She later said that she felt George and Dinah only communicated with one another when they were talking about their careers.

"If you look for reasons behind their troubles, I think one is to be found in the fact that George is much more capable than people give him credit for being.

"I feel that it must be very difficult for a man to live in true compatibility with a woman who is much more successful than he is. Mrs. Montgomery must have wanted very much for him to do something really important, because she obviously loved him greatly.''

Three months later, George had finished with the picture and brought it back to the United States. It was not released until 1962, and by then, the Dinah/George Montgomery marriage had split wide open. In fact, a divorce was granted to Dinah in May, less than a month after *Samar* opened in New York.

It was too late to patch up the marriage. Gossip columnists attributed the breakup to an alleged ''affair'' between George and his Israeli leading lady. She denied it vehemently.

The picture didn't do badly. Howard Thompson, writing in *The New York Times*, said, ''Director-producer-star George Montgomery rates credit for pluckily whacking this little adventure out of the Philippine jungle with a machete. Mr. Montgomery is also the co-scenarist of a story about the organized flight of a penal colony in the mountains, away from Spanish colonialism. It's 1870, says the prologue.

''On a frank, adventure level, the picture pivots in a kind of sweaty masculinity. This is Mr. Montgomery's limber directing above and beyond his rather bare-chested performance as an American physician. In addition to having a directorial knack for crowd scenes, he is also blessed with a first-rate color photographer, Emmanual Rojas. The picture looks genuine Philippines-made, down to the dart headhunter palm, and the Montgomery-Rojas team really goes to town in the battle sequences.

''If the script substitutes briskness for depth, we'll buy it—along with Ziva Rodann and Joan O'Brien for looks. Mico Minardos does well as a tough Spanish Army officer.''

Warner Brothers didn't make much money on the first showing, but did pick up money on the eventual television rights. *Movies on TV* said:

"Commandant of a penal colony refuses to bow to his strict superiors, breaks with the administration and leads his people through the jungles to freedom. highly interesting, unusual story well done; rugged adventure fare."

As early as 1960, Dinah had been thinking deeply and distractedly about her disintegrating marriage. It wasn't only the fact that George wanted to go off into the jungles and make pictures. It had become apparent to many friends of the Montgomerys that for some time George was straying from the marital reservation as well. Still a handsome, virile, and likable man, he had no reason to lack for female companions. And with his wife putting sixty hours a week into her career, there were plenty of moments when George was quite free to do whatever he wanted to do with his time.

It was Dinah's decision not to involve herself in a divorce. It would be destructive to her children, as well as to herself and to George. On a professional level, there was the fact that the public relations of divorce was not good, even in an America that had begun to tolerate almost any kind of marital shakeup.

"I care very much how people feel," Dinah said. "I am sensitive to any response they give me when I perform. This is the miracle of silent communication. I never cease to be in awe of it or grateful to it for some of the highest, most glowing moments of my life."

Dinah apparently started thinking very seriously about divorce during the Christmas holidays of 1960. The day after Christmas, George left for the Philippines to make the first adventure picture. He was gone three months.

The two of them found it increasingly difficult to communicate with one another, hiding their true feelings in myriad details about production values, scenic shots, and financial entanglements. That was the reason George's letters were like reports to the chairman of the board rather than letters to the woman he loved.

But by June, 1961, it was apparent to them both that things could not go on as they had been going.

"Friends believe that during a brief vacation in Palm Springs, six months before the public announcement was made, they agreed to part," wrote Carl Schroeder in a national magazine.

However, Dinah did not make the final decision as to the exact date she would announce the separation until late in 1961.

In June, 1961, Dinah kept the children in Palm Springs. George returned to the Beverly Hills house. There was no one around except for several of the household staff. One of them was Ruth Wenzel, an aspiring actress. She wanted to impress George in any way she could. She thought he could help her get into show business.

In the solitude of the almost empty house, she knew her chance had come. And she knew just how to impress her handsome employer, "I swam with him," she said. "And we sat very close. I thought he was going to kiss me, but then the doorbell rang."

The interruption was only temporary. Next day, the two were out on the edge of the swimming pool again, and George put sunburn lotion on her back. According to Ruth's statement later, she and he had relations several times between June and August, 1961.

When Dinah and the children returned, Wenzel said, "George told me he would never get close to me again, that he was getting upset and couldn't stand it anymore." George ordered her to move to Pasadena. He said he would come there to see her.

Obviously such a relationship could never be kept secret. Dinah certainly suspected something. Whatever happened, on November 29, 1961, Ruth Wenzel was fired from the Montgomery household. Within hours Dinah announced her impending separation from George.

The decision to separate was made on the day of

her weekly television show. She told George it was all over before she left for the studio in Burbank. George packed his bags and left the house. Dinah took the two bewildered children with her to the NBC Studios, and after the telecast was made the three of them drove away to an unnamed hideaway.

All she said to her associates was, "I have to get away. It's just something I can't talk about to anyone."

Hollywood's "perfect marriage" was over.

9

"Didn't You
Used to be
Dinah Shore?"

The divorce decree that severed the marriage of Dinah Shore to George Montgomery was granted on May 10, 1962.

Dinah was a rich woman, one of the most famous in the world, but in private life she was lonely and confused. She had reached the pinnacle of public adulation, and her career could only be described as fabulous.

Yet in her private life she had lost the center of her family's existence—her husband and the father of her children. Now she had two children to bring up all by herself. Except for her sister and brother-in-law, she was alone.

"I had always promised myself that I would be a good mother and wife—and life had proved that I wasn't. It was sad truth to face."

Even the words she had uttered in pleading for the divorce seemed hollow and unreal. "My husband was away for three months at a stretch in 1959, three months in 1960, three months in 1961, and often shorter periods.

"I asked him, in fact urged him, not to leave, but he went anyway."

At other times, she had told the judge, he was at home, but still absent in spirit.

"We would have guests for dinner and George would spend the whole time talking on the phone."

What was the point of explaining that the very unreal atmosphere of the home—with the wife a woman at the zenith of her public career, and the husband a man struggling to keep alive in a tough profession—had helped create and widen the rift between their private lives?

Could it be explained?

The settlement in its fashion was as cold-blooded and heartless as most divorce settlements are: for Dinah the Beverly Hills home worth about a quarter of a million dollars; for Dinah the children; for George "reasonable visitation rights."

She was despondent over the split-up, but it was too late do anything about it. Nor was she sure what she could have done about it even if she had tried to work something out sooner. The paths of their lives had simply veered too far apart from each other to ever come together again.

Other chances came into her life. The Chevvy show had been rolling along for ten years. In 1961, when the trials and tribulations of her private life began to take their toll on her stamina, she had decided to leave it for good. It ended in 1961.

In fact, many of her friends blamed the stress and strain of the show's long run for her personal woes. One described her as always being "terribly uptight during the Chevvy period." Undoubtedly the burden of carrying the show and all its problems like an incubus on her shoulder contributed to her breakup with George.

When the Chevvy show finally wound down after 599 performances, Dinah Shore found herself almost at loose ends. But in a way the freedom was a godsend. Now at last she had plenty of time to do what she had always wanted to do.

She moved down to Palm Springs and began to play all the tennis she hadn't been able to play while her show was on the air. And the two children were around to keep her company. Nor was it as if George Montgomery was completely out of her life, either. He did everything he could to help out with Melissa and Jody.

"They both have great respect for each other," an associate said, reviewing the situation after the divorce. "George is a big, rough guy, but basically a gentleman. Dinah is first, last and always a lady in the Southern tradition—and ladies do not cry in public."

"I'm going to take a one-year sabbatical," she told her friends. "Just lounge around in blue jeans in the sun. I'm going to spend some time with the children and just think a little. I want to reappraise the whole picture of my life. You know—do you really have to work that hard?"

In addition, she took up golf once again, enjoying the game now as she had never been able to before. "My score would look much better as a bowling score," she said ruefully during her first months of practice, but she began to improve dramatically.

It was largely as a result of her love affair with golf that summer in Palm Springs that the status of Ladies' Professional Golf was advanced to a considerable degree.

Even though Dinah had never considered herself much of a Women's Libber, for a long time she had been miffed at the fact that women in golf did not make anywhere near the amount of money that men in golf

did. For example, a typical PGA tournament for men
like the Bob Hope Desert Classic would net the winner
an amount that was equal to an entire season for a
woman golfer.

Or, to look at it another way, in 1971, money
leader Jack Nicklaus cleared $244,490 in the PGA. In
the same year, money leader Kathy Whitworth made
only $41,181—just one-sixth as much!

It was Dinah's intention to try somehow to increase
the winner's purse for women golfers. And it was
television, she thought, that could do the trick. Golf was
visual—beautiful grass, trees, the open sky, and plenty
of celebrities walking around, playing and observing. It
was a natural for television. And, since the advent of
color, television had already made golf a household
word for most Americans.

Colgate put up the money to sponsor a tournament
for women in 1970, a meeting that from then on was
known as the Colgate–Dinah Shore–Women's Circle
Ladies' Professional Golf Association Tournament,
held in Palm Springs at the Mission Hills Country Club.
If nothing else, it was probably the most lengthy title
ever given to any golf tournament.

From the moment it started, it attracted women
golfers in large numbers. Television coverage drew
viewers all over America. In its first few years the tournament made $2 billion through the sale of golf prod-
ucts to women. And in 1973 the purse was $139,000
—three times what Kathy Whitworth had made all year
in 1971.

By 1976 the Dinah Shore Tournament was pulling a
higher television audience rating than the Men's United
States Open! And there was 15,000 in the gallery
watching the Dinah Shore Tourney in Palm Springs!

But the proof of the pudding was in the numbers:
in 1975 money leader Jack Nicklaus made $323,149; his
counterpart in the LPGA, Sandra Palmer, made

$94,805, above one third. The money differential had been cut in half.

It was Dinah Shore's name, her determination, and her enthusiasm for sports that got the tournament off the ground, and gave impetus to others. She was given the Achievement in Life Award in 1973 by the All-American Collegiate Golf Association at a dinner in New York at the Waldorf-Astoria.

She came to love the game. And because she was Dinah, she liked to look the best she could when she played. She confessed to a friend that she had two golf outfits ready for each tournament she was playing.

"I'm never sure before I wake up the morning of the game which one I'm going to wear—the fat outfit or the thin outfit. The decision usually hinges on how much I have exercised the day before or how much I misbehaved at the table the night before."

One thing she learned, she said, was to stay away from size 6 golfers. They made her look bulky. As she put it, "They destroy you."

Another little ploy was to wear an outfit one size too large. "It hangs on you, and a lot of people watching the game at home will say, 'Gosh, it looks like she's losing weight!' "

In fact, keeping her weight down was always something Dinah didn't need to worry about. She burned off so much energy that she really didn't need to go on stringent diets.

"An old man I met once gave me the secret of staying in trim. He was very round and very jolly and always had a bagel in his mouth. But he knew what to do even if he didn't do it.

"Every morning after you awaken, and each evening before you retire, you stand naked before a three-way mirror. You look at yourself, and then you ask yourself: "Do I really want to look like this?' "

In spite of all the publicity she got for her own golf

tournament and the hours of coverage on television,
Dinah was never able to join any of the country clubs in
Los Angeles. "They won't let me join," she explained,
"because I'm a single woman! Apparently the feeling is
that a girl who isn't married is a potential home-
wrecker."

It might have been great for her ego, but it was not
great for her competitive instincts.

The last time it happened, she said, she went home
and washed her hair she was so mad. "When some
women get upset, they go shopping," she laughed.
"Others take a bath. Still others crawl in bed. But when
I'm mad, I give myself a shampoo and set."

Her keen interest in sports helped her personal life
somewhat, taking her mind off her shattered marriage,
but Dinah was definitely a family girl. Many of her
friends were advising her to remarry, although she was
hesitant about it at first.

One of her oldest and dearest friends suggested that
she marry him.

"I'd love to," she said brightly, "but you do have a
wife and two children."

"A mere detail."

"I know. I found that out," said Dinah with a
touch of irony.

With her leisure time, Dinah was able to increase
the frequence of her tennis game from two or three
times a week to every day. It was her infatuation with
tennis that led her to a crucial and traumatic relationship that seemed to be all part and parcel of her divorce
from George and her everlasting quest for the "ideal
marriage."

In Palm Springs she met Maurice F. Smith, a
building contractor who lived there and who played
tennis rather well. Dinah and he were constant singles
opponents and constant doubles partners.

Although Dinah had learned through long and bitter experience that there was no real magic in marriage,

she had always dreamed that there was an ideal relationship somewhere out there in the blue.

"I just know it's there," she said once. "I really do. I've seen one or two or three really happy marriages, where people give to each other, respect each other, live in terms of each other. Seeing even a few makes you realize, God, it must be possible. What a wonderful way of living and thinking and feeling. You know, to be able to give and take selflessly."

It was tempting to her to visualize herself somehow involved in an "ideal" companionship once again. On May 26, 1963, just a few days over a year after her divorce from George was final, Dinah married her tennis partner, becoming Mrs. Maurice F. Smith.

The marriage was a fiasco. It lasted less than a year. By May 10, 1964, Dinah and Maurice called it off and she filed for divorce.

"I couldn't make an independent decision," she toldthe judge, "because my husband criticized everything I did so much." She said that she had been subjected to "extreme anxiety" by the actions of her husband.

The divorce was granted.

By the time the traumatic experience of the second divorce was in the past, Dinah secretly vowed to herself that she would never marry again. There was something about the state of marriage that didn't seem to work out for her.

George Montgomery was not having an easy time of his life as a divorcé, either. During the time of Dinah's marriage to Maurice Smith, George was still going with Ruth Wenzel. However, he soon broke up with her and began seeing other women.

On the night of August 27, 1963, he brought home an airline stewardess with whom he was acquainted, only to be confronted on the front porch by Ruth Wenzel. While the stewardess watched, George and Ruth began arguing loudly. Finally George ordered her off the property and unlocked the door to go inside with the stewardess.

Ruth pushed past them, rushed into the bedroom, and reached under George's pillow, pulling out a .38 caliber revolver she had hidden there. George grabbed her hand and wrestled with the gun. During the struggle, the gun went off, the shot barely missing George's head.

Finally he subdued her and telephoned the police, who took her off with them and booked her.

Later, investigating officers found a note she had left at her apartment. "I am planning to kill George Montgomery, and then myself, of course . . . I don't know if I'm able to kill him . . . I couldn't do it before.

"I told him once that I don't want him to go out with those stupid glamour girls. They will ruin his reputation."

Meanwhile, Dinah was having her own set of troubles, mostly concerning the two children. Melissa Ann, for example, had become what might be called a "problem." She took to telephoning for taxicabs to come pick her up at the house and drive her around the city on mysterious excursions. When her mother questioned her, she became very evasive.

She had an almost ambivalent attitude about her mother. On one visit to an amusement park with Dinah, she became angry at a group of autograph seekers who were pushing her while they tried to get to her mother.

Finally she backed off and screamed at them. "Go away! She's not Dinah Shore today. She's my mother!"

That didn't help Dinah's image with her fans. But at the same time, it showed Dinah that her relationship with her daughter was always subject to outside pressures that were liable to injure it irreparably.

Melissa and a friend from school once visited the friend's house, a small place in a very modest neighborhood. There were children running around the streets and yelling at one another.

Melissa looked longingly at the small house, compared it in her mind to her own $250,000 home nearby, and said wistfully:

"I wish I lived in your house."

She once wrote: "I wanted Dinah Shore to please get out of my life and leave me alone to enjoy my mother."

Because of the fact that she had so much spare time, Dinah began to practice her oil painting once again. She had always enjoyed it, and now she decided to practice in earnest. Melissa took up the hobby with her. The two of them started working together for hours at a time. In fact, their work was exhibited in several places.

Occasionally, Dinah took on short-term singing engagements, doing a half dozen shows for television, or a six-week stint at the Riviera Hotel in Las Vegas.

When she went on jobs like that, she always took Melissa and Jody along with her, accompanied by a tutor who kept them up in their schoolwork until they returned to their classrooms in a Beverly Hills public school.

One of the reasons Dinah cut down on her work was her own peace of mind and the state of her health.

"All the stories about my incredible vitality are somewhat exaggerated," she said. "It's true that I have a 'second wind' that enables me to work intensely for as much as sixty hours a week, but there are many times when I am terribly tired and long to go home to stay with my family for keeps."

And she learned finally that a parent should be around her children all the time. "After the divorce, George helped when he could, but he was just not around enough. Still, the children have turned out to be well balanced. They're protective of me, and I of them, and we're all the stronger for it."

She had always found it terribly difficult to enforce discipline on the two children—something that George rarely had trouble doing. When Melissa graduated from high school, Dinah promised her that if she got a B average, she would be able to have a car. Melissa tried, but simply couldn't get really good marks.

Dinah broke down and got her the car anyway.

"I had told her," Dinah reported, "that she would have to make her own choice and then live with it. That she had to build a sense of responsibility, and when she earned the car, she could have it. And then I saw all her friends with cars and how hard it was for her to get around in this inflated Beverly Hills atmosphere—and I got her one!"

Dinah still played dates around the country. During the time of her divorce from George, and then her divorce from Maurice Smith, it was difficult to put together singing schedules for her. Dinah now had a press agent named Charles Pomerantz. Pomerantz said, "About the only song she could do at that point that wouldn't have a direct meaning was 'The Star-Spangled Banner.' " For example, Pomerantz pointed out, one program had "It's So Nice to Have a Man Around the House," and "Hello, Young Lovers." And there were more. All those were no-no's.

About this time Dinah was visiting New York where she and a friend got into a taxicab. She was wearing dark glasses to protect her eyes from the sun. But that didn't keep the cabby from peering again and again at her in the rearview mirror.

"Hey," he said. "Aren't you . . .?" The cabby hesitated. "No, no, wait! Don't tell me, don't tell me!" Dinah waited. After about three minutes, the cab driver's face lit up and he turned around and pointed at her, shouting loudly and triumphantly, "Doris Day!"

She had cut down on her schedule, but, she thought, not quite that much! Nevertheless, her public image was eroding. Several months later she was getting off the jetliner in Los Angeles, looking for a cab, when she bumped into an old friend from her television days.

"Hey," he said, "didn't you used to be Dinah Shore?"

The children always came first. But in 1969, Melissa, who was twenty-one years old, became engaged to a young actor and producer named David Lee Buck. On March 16, Melissa was married to him at Dinah's Beverly Hills home. Everyone was there—Dinah, Jody, Aunt Bessie and Uncle Morsey (As Dr. Maurice Seligman was known by the children)—that is, everyone but George. He was in Africa on a film he was producing.

After the festivities were all over and Melissa and David on their way to their honeymoon, Jody went back to Connecticut, where he was enrolled in a private school.

Dinah was suddenly, for the first time in a long while, all alone.

The 1960's, a most traumatic decade for America, was finally drawing to a close. The bombings, the assassinations, the overseas war—all these manifestations of inner turmoil and conflict—were finally about to wind down.

With its maladjustments and paranoia, the Sixties had brought a new thing to the country—an obsession with self-examination, with self-flagellation, with probing to the core of the American persona. One of the more harmless symptoms of this need for self-examination was the astounding proliferation of the late-night "talk shows" on television.

Johnny Carson, Merv Griffin, Mike Douglas—a host of hosts, you might say—became mavens of the American psyche. Sickened by the news in the media, people turned more and more to these exchanges of small talk among bright and witty personalities for catharsis.

And they apparently got it.

It was Henry Jaffe who actually came up with the

big idea. It took some finesse, because Jaffe knew how
Dinah Shore felt about going back to work on
television. But he knew how her mind worked. She had
often enough voiced her opinion to him that she would
never again do another variety show.

Sure, Jaffe said, a *variety* show was too much for
her. He didn't have that kind of show in mind.

"But now your kids are on their way, Dinah. You
have no commitments except an occasional singing
engagement. Let me tell you an idea I've been turning
over in my mind."

Dinah blanched. She really didn't want to give up
her tennis and golf.

"You're intelligent, well read, warm with people."

She sat there, waiting. She knew Jaffe had some
scheme she didn't want to hear about.

"Why not do a daytime television show in which
your guests would be invited simply to enjoy themselves, with or without heavy talk?"

"You mean a daytime talk show?" Dinah shook
her head.

"You'll only have to work two days a week. You'll
have plenty of time for tennis."

Dinah turned the idea over in her mind.

"I misled her a little," Jaffe later admitted. "There
were two days of filming. That didn't include the
preparation and the script meetings."

After some soul-searching, Dinah finally agreed,
but only after Jaffe had really put the pressure on her.
Once they got their heads together, the ideas came up
like bubbles of champagne.

On her Chevvy show, Dinah had got more mail
about the clothes she wore than the songs she sang. She
was realistic enough to know that her appearance was
even more important than her singing skills.

"I may have Galanos or Donald Davies pin a dress
on me while we talk," she mused aloud as they made
notes about future bits.

What they came up with was an "open-end show." It would entertain and teach at the same time. It would tell women how to stay attractive, young, and beautiful. It would encourage and show them how to cook special recipes. It would tell them how to diet, how to take care of their husbands and children, how to sew clothes and apply makeup.

And so the format took shape and the date was set and Dinah still had severe misgivings.

"I don't know why I came back to television," she moaned to critic Kay Gardella. "I think it's the stupidest thing I've ever done!

"Actually, I live a pretty full life as a woman. I play tennis, do needlepoint, cook, love my music and generally keep busy in several directions, including painting."

The show opened in August, 1970. *Dinah's Place* had a set that was a duplicate of Dinah's own Beverly Hills home, the one that had been designed and built by George Montgomery. The viewer felt that he or she was coming right into Dinah's house to meet other guests.

It had a "warm, tastefully decorated set," in Kay Gardella's words.

The simple set had great versatility, too. It could be used as a living room and as a kitchen, with the stove and counter off to one side. In fact, a major part of the show's gimmick was to let Dinah be in the kitchen, making a favorite recipe as she chatted with her guests.

Because of the informality of the set, and Dinah's own warm personality, the viewer—primarily the housewife—was treated to a kind of special visit away from home without having to move from her armchair.

Most of the critics liked the show.

"Miss Shore made it all informal and friendly, showing a domestic ease that is apparently to be the show's premise," said *Variety*. "The sets are fine, as are the prospects of this variety format."

Not all, however, agreed. *Women's Wear Daily*, in

the person of someone signing the name "Joyce Needleman," wrote, "Dinah Shore's new daytime television show, nationwide on NBC—at 10 A.M., in time for the morning coffee break—is another one of TV's mindless, banal, superficial time-killers.

"Dinah conducts a trite question-and-answer interview with a famous guest star, throws in a song or two and ends with her well-worn lip-smacking kiss."

Needleman thought the guests were more professional than the hostess. "Her guests . . . relieve the tension Dinah creates by her forced, artificial casualness. The guests are really much more relaxed than the hostess.

"When TV producers and personalities learn that a growing number of women who stay home to keep house and mind the children are concerned with topical issues . . . and do enjoy the art of thinking, perhaps we'll get a stimulating woman's show rather than another run-of-the-mill presentation like *Dinah's Place.*"

It was 1970, and the turbulent 1960's were not really quite out of sight yet.

Kay Gardella wrote in the New York *Daily News:* "The friendly, outgoing singer hasn't lost her television touch. It promises to be a relaxed, easy-to-take offering."

It was a hit with the public right from the start.

Yet Dinah was trying to figure out how to get out of her commitment for weeks after it began.

"I didn't know what I was doing," she said, "and they threw some real curves at me."

A psychologist who specialized in saving marriages spent most of his time describing—quite graphically, with most explicit pantomime—a case history of a wife who got upset when her husband fondled her while she was peeling potatoes.

Dinah, embarrassed and repelled by the psychologist's lack of taste, smiled nevertheless, and nodded: "Well, that does sound like fun."

Bishop Fulton J. Sheen spent most of his allotted time simply staring at Dinah hypnotically.

"I could only sit there and stare back," she said, "which didn't make for much audience excitement."

Martha Mitchell, the wife of the Attorney General, admitted to Dinah that she had once advocated that parents send their draft-age sons to Canada and said she wished her son was there instead of in Vietnam.

Barry Goldwater stated that the government really didn't have a constitutional right to draft anyone during peacetime, or even during a war.

Hubert Humphrey, fussing about in Dinah's television kitchen, where the show was playing, burned himself accidentally on a hot pot, cried out, "Oh, my God!" and then smote himself and groaned, "Well, I just blew the Bible belt."

Viewers who had become tired of the bloated and inane conversations on television's late-night talk shows began to tune in more and more to *Dinah's Place*. The success of the show obviously came about because of Dinah's own ideas about what such a show should constitute.

"We don't have the time or luxury to probe," she told an interviewer. "What we are is a *do* show, not a *talk* show. Almost everyone who comes on has something he wants to do. Ethel Kennedy played the piano. Joanne Woodward did some beautiful needlepoint. Cliff Robertson made a linguine. Leslie Uggams made sweet potato pie. Burt Lancaster made a perfect Italian spaghetti sauce. Senator Muskie hynotized a lobster. Frank Sinatra showed up to cook spaghetti and to sing."

The toughest part of the show, Dinah confessed, was in the laying out of the recipes. The audience tended to think of Dinah's Place as a cooking show.

"I don't like to dispel that notion, because it has enhanced my myth, but it really isn't a cooking show at all. In fact, the cooking is quite simply an obstacle course."

But an important obstacle course. After the show's first season had concluded, Dinah gathered the new recipes she had tried on the show—many of them from celebrity guests—and put them together in a cookbook for Doubleday titled *Someone's in the Kitchen with Dinah*.

"I never got a standing ovation for a pot roast," she admitted, "but it feels like one when guests go back for seconds. The book is the result of my career in the kitchen and just enjoying good food everywhere in the world."

One summer, she said, she had actually eaten her way across the continent from restaurant to restaurant. It was a gastronomic tour par excellence, with a good friend.

"Cooking can be a great adventure, and learning about it can be, too. I gathered every recipe in my book and I tested every single one. In fact, I've got extra six pounds to prove it."

No less an expert in gourmet dining than Craig Claiborne, the food maven of *The New York Times*, said of the book:

"Dinah is the author of a fascinating, relatively small, but first-rate cookbook," he wrote. "It is a personal, well-varied book scattered with anecdotes and easy-to-follow recipes."

Quite an accolade, from the *Times'* food master.

"I like the informal flavor of the morning show," Dinah said. "And I get a chance to sing. We do the entire week of shows in two days. We even tape an extra show just in case I want a long weekend vacation. That way I'm carried on a wave of enthusiasm from guest to guest, and that way I have some time to recover and get in some tennis."

Enthusiasm had always been Dinah's middle name, anyway. Now, after the recent slumps in her life—the end of her marriage to George Montgomery, followed quickly by the fiasco of her second marriage and divorce—she had something to get her mind off her troubles.

Besides, Dinah had always prided herself on her ability to take the worst reverses life had to offer her. "I have what must be a growing ability to roll with the punches," she said. "I find I can put down any guilt that might come out of constant self-examination. I *feel* so many marvelous things, I wouldn't trade for all the soul-searching in the world!"

On the show she generally avoided heavy and serious discussions of religion or politics.

"When people appear with me, they are guests in my home, almost literally. And in my home—even if I'm at odds with them—I will never try to beat guests down.

"I can't stand to embarrass anyone, even my own kids. My first reaction when people say something embarrassing is to help them cover. I admire people with strong convictions. I listen to all sides here, and I've learned that people with real convictions aren't that far apart in basic philosophy. It's their way of going about it that is different.

"That's why I can talk comfortably with people who hold totally divergent views. What I don't question is their sincerity, and that's what moves me—the fact that they truly, honestly believe."

The first season of the show included such different personalities as Joe Namath, Mario Puzo, Efrem Zimbalist, Jr., David Janssen, Burt Bacharach, Linus Pauling, Rita Hayworth, Adele Davis, Spiro Agnew, Hubert Humphrey, and Gloria Steinem.

Commenting on Gloria Steinem's appearance, Dinah said that the studio audience was loaded that day with "women who had this terrible anger toward men."

Dinah observed, "I don't understand this violence. We're in the world together, you know. There are so many myths connected with the relationship between men and women. If women have been exploited, it's been a collaborative effort and not a giant conspiracy on the part of men. Being a homemaker is a lovely, marvelous role and only denigrating if you yourself make it that way."

About Women's Liberation she always had mixed feelings, anyway. "I was always an emancipated woman, and I certainly think Germaine Greer and Gloria Steinem are doing a marvelous job."

But as a wife and mother, she always thought that having a man go out and fight for her was a bargain she wouldn't want to forgo. She could never understand why some women seemed to think they had the wrong end of the deal. "In fact, they've got the best end."

Dinah always thought that when a woman worked, she should be paid the same as a man, because food and clothing was just as expensive for the woman. But if she threatened a man's job, then she was depriving another family of a breadwinner.

"Some of the Women's Lib ladies we've had on the show have shocked me," she said. "They talked of men as though they weren't human, something from another planet, the enemy.

"I deplore that. It's always been a man's world, and it probably always will be. I don't want to change that. All of my career, on radio, in recording studios, in films and on television, men have made the decisions for me, and they've usually been the right ones."

As for Dinah's private life, she felt the same way about men. "I owe everything, my success and the degree of happiness I've achieved, to men. Why, as a woman, should I be ashamed to say that?"

A friend of hers, close to her for many years, once said of her: "I've never met a man who wasn't moved by her warmth. She makes a man *feel* like a man."

That statement always pleased Dinah. It summed up what she had learned about life.

"Being a woman," she said, "is only in terms of a man. That sounds terribly old-fashioned, doesn't it? I'm an individual person, and yet I think of my life as incomplete unless it's in terms of a man. So I guess my life hasn't been complete, you know. It just never worked out that way.

"But I still believe that if a man and woman can live in terms of each other, there is great strength in the relationship. That's what makes a marriage. You can't go into it shrugging and saying, 'Well, if it doesn't work, we'll do something else.' "

Her concept of male-female relationships was quite different from the Women's Lib idea.

"I think a friendship between a man and woman is beautiful. To be truly in love with each other, they have to be friends—and be able to share weaknesses as well as strengths."

Her own marriage had taught her something. "You build fantasies and you put people on pedestals and they put you on one. You endow them with those qualities you'd like them to have—and then both of you try to live up to the image. But the pictures you paint are one-dimensional, and it takes a long time to face up to reality. When you do, it hurts. It takes a while."

Nevertheless, she still believed in love. "I wouldn't change it, I really wouldn't. Even what hurts. I think I've benefited enormously. I've learned a lot about people and about myself, and I think I've had better experiences because I believe in people, and people know I do.

"We're all affected by the thinking the young people have put on us today—that there's a terrible impermanence in the world. But don't forget, we're doing something about almost everything, and I can't help believing that we're making enormous strides. We grow from pain. If everything had been just rosy and wonderful for me, I would have been a vegetable."

And she was still trying to work out in her own

mind a way to have a good relationship with a man after her two unsuccessful marriages.

"We all carry a little facade around with us, an image of ourselves that we don't want to chip away for fear of losing love or respect or whatever it is we need.

"But to be able to have some of these self-delusions broken down and faced up to and have somebody else share them with you is a marvelous thing—to enjoy companionship without fear of judgment."

And she was going to meet a man soon who would put all these preconceptions and ideals to the supreme test. When he came on the scene, she was ready for him.

As the show continued from day to day, Dinah began to be more confident of the way to do it. She became somewhat more challenging, using her low-key interviewing technique to draw people out to say things they had never said before in public.

She never ran out of guests. One scientist who had refused an invitation to *Dinah's Place* because he considered it "pablum" changed his mind after appearing on a panel show with Dinah. When he discovered that she read a wide range of newspapers, magazines, and books, and could talk in depth about most current affairs, he willingly signed up.

And she got guests from friends she found in such varied places as swimming pools and tennis courts.

"Tennis is the booker of all time," she said once. "I get to know a lot of people because I have the best court in Hollywood—and the best food!"

Dinah was a first-class player. The only time she ever came a cropper on the court was when she was playing doubles with Spiro Agnew, during the time he was Vice-President.

"I still don't know how it happened," she said later. "I was the Vice-President's partner, and I was at the net with my back to him when he served."

Whatever happened, an instant later Agnew's ten-

nis ball was in Dinah's right eye. The smash was so hard
Dinah had a black eye for three days.

"Yes, I'm a Democrat," Dinah laughed, "but that
had nothing to do with it. Did it?"

She recovered. Agnew later appeared on her show.

"Honest," Dinah said later, "I think it's safer
playing with Pancho Gonzalez. With Pancho, you serve
the ball and run."

Dinah was always serious about her tennis playing.
She once told a writer, "I can sing before ten thousand
people, cook before ten million viewers on my show,
but put me on a tennis court with two hundred people in
the stands and I absolutely freeze."

Her game was improving so much that sometimes
she tended to become a bit overconfident. One of her
constant companions on the court was Burt Bacharach,
the songwriter. Burt loved to play singles, and so did
Dinah; most everyone else in their set liked doubles.

"I was scheduled to make a trip to Japan on a
singing tour," Dinah recalled, "and I wanted to take
my drummer, Mark Stevens, along with me. Burt
Bacharach wanted Mark to stay in town for the West
Coast production of Burt's *Promises, Promises*."

The two tennis buffs got into a yelling argument
over Mark one day.

"I'll give you anything, but not Mark," Dinah told
Burt. She pointed out that she couldn't possibly go to
Japan and try to sing with all new musicians. She
pleaded with him, but to no avail.

The upshot of the argument was that Dinah and
Burt agreed to play tennis for Mark. Whoever won got
him. It was like one of those old Western poker or gun
duels.

"I was sure I'd win," Dinah said. "I even went to
Mark and told him not worry, that he'd surely go to
Japan."

Dinah played a good game, but it wasn't as good as

Burt's. Looking back on it, she realized that she had been so sure she would win that she had relaxed herself righ out of the match.

"Whenever Mark saw me after that, he always reminded me that I had lost him a trip to the Orient," Dinah said ruefully.

Although she and Burt were great tennis fans and good neighbors, they never really discussed music too much. Dinah was used to singing numbers that were rather old-fashioned and straight. Burt wrote very new and off-beat numbers with shifting modes and tricky rhythms. The two were "light years apart" in style, as one friend said.

Dinah finally persuaded Burt to teach her one of his most beautiful songs, "One Less Bell to Answer." She studied hard and did exactly as he told her to do under his careful tutelage. It was a lesson she learned painstakingly and meticulously. She knew herself how different from her own type of song his was.

"I learned every bit of it *right*," Dinah said.

Some time later she was at a party given by her friend Molly Parness Livingston. Someone asked her to sing. There was no professional accompanist there, Ticker Freeman being away on a short vacation.

Guest Burt Bacharach finally agreed to back Dinah on the piano. And because it was Burt, Dinah chose to sing his own lovely tune, "One Less Bell To Answer."

At first she was frightened that she might do the number wrong. Yet when she started in, she could see that Burt was playing and moving his head slowly back and forth as she sang.

"I'm really getting through to him," Dinah thought. They had been through the number together many times at Dinah's house, but now she knew she was doing it justice. She had finally turned the tide.

Later on, at the Copa, when the two of them were guests to close singer Dionne Warwick's engagement,

Dinah boldly announced to Burt that she was going to record his song, "One Less Bell to Answer."

"I've never sung it wrong," she said.

Burt looked startled. "You've never sung it right!" he retorted.

"But . . ." Dinah stuttered. "That night at Molly's dinner party, when you played for me, you sat there shaking your head back and forth in approval!"

"No," said Burt, correcting her. "That wasn't what I meant at all. I was shaking my head and whispering to myself, 'Wrong, wrong, wrong'!"

The success of her talk show brought people flocking once again to her home in Beverly Hills. Soon it became known as "Dinah's Bar and Grill." Located only a few blocks from the Beverly Hills Hotel, where the most celebrated hangout in Hollywood, the famed Polo Lounge, was located, Dinah's house became the gathering place for all the big names in show business after the Lounge was locked up for the night.

People like Danny Kaye, Danny Thomas, Liz and Richard Burton, Dean Martin, Jerry Lewis, and Frank Sinatra would head there to eat and drink and jive with Dinah.

One of the first people Dinah had on her show was her old antagonist Frank Sinatra—whom she had known since early WNEW days. She had him cook one of his Italian dishes. "People don't know what a marvelous cook he is," she said.

As for Vice-President Agnew, when she finally got him on the show for the first time, she sang a song to his rather laborious piano playing. They tried "Sophisticated Lady," Duke Ellington's classic tune. Dinah started out and did about a line of the lyrics, and then cried out, "This is Jane Powell's key!"

They then tried "Tea for Two." It wasn't much better. When she found she couldn't make it, she gasped out, "This is Robert Goulet's key!"

That was the end of the session.

Dinah had not yet really given up on men, although she had been married and divorced twice.

"I have always leaned on men," she told an interviewer, "even though it looks otherwise. I think that's why I chose singing, because it's not the highly competitive field becoming an actress might be.

"If it's your style they like, then you're the one they want, not somebody else. Besides, as I said before, I'd miss a great deal in my life if I ever stopped singing.

"It also places me in the wonderful position of not having to take sides where men are concerned. It blends so beautifully with being a woman. But as much as I've always wanted a career, I've always secretly envied women who are loved and supported by men.

"When you're in my position, you're never sure they love you for what you are or for what you accomplish. But as schizophrenic as it sounds, I still have to go on doing what I'm doing—singing."

But she had never really stopped looking for that ideal man. On one of her early talk shows she signed up an actor who had never made it big and was still struggling to do so.

His name was Burt Reynolds.

10

The Anatomy
of a
Love Affair

Burt Reynolds came from Waycross, Georgia, where he was born on February 11, 1936. His name was actually Burt Reynolds, Jr., but he was called "Buddy" at home to distinguish him from his father.

His mother's side of the family was mostly of Italian descent, but his father's mother was a full-blooded Cherokee Indian. With his brother and sister he grew up in Waycross and in West Palm Beach, Florida, where the family moved soon afterward.

Buddy's father became the chief of police of West Palm Beach and served in that capacity for most of Buddy's younger years. Actually, his father had been a cowpoke during his youth, but had become an officer of the law out of necessity when the beef business in Georgia went sour during the Depression.

Buddy Reynolds grew up in a family that believed in discipline to a point that not even the slightest deviation from the rigid rules of the house was condoned. The boy was by nature a rebel. When he went up against his father, all he got was trouble.

His father had no scruples about what is now called "corporal punishment," but was then called "the flat of the hand applied to the curve of the bottom." Buddy was constantly on the carpet, constantly being slapped about, and constantly running away to join sea pirates, the marines, and even the Indians.

In 1951 he got as far away as South Carolina, where he was picked up on a vagrancy charge. The law put him in a cell and let him cool his heels there for a week, after which they shipped him home.

"How are you, boy?" his father asked him coolly.

Buddy didn't like his father's attitude at all, and moved out. He lived for almost a year with the family of a girlfriend, just to prove something to his father. What he was trying to prove he never really found out. Nor did his father.

At school he wasn't called "Buddy" any more. He was called "Greaseball" or "Mullet." The latter was in reference to the Rivera Beach fisherman's neighborhood where he lived.

"I thought it was 'Rivera Beach' until I was in high school," he recalled once. "I wasn't much of a reader." At least, he liked everybody to *think* he wasn't.

As for acting, the stage was never "in his blood," as they used to say, but he continuing escapades with the gang and his confrontations with his father gave him an opportunity to practice exactly the same kind of deceit employed in the acting profession simply to save his own hide. However, he did play some dramatic roles in high school.

But he felt that the stage was for weirdos. Buddy loved football. He was one of the toughest of the high school stars, and he played fullback for the home team. He loved the rough and tumble of contact sports and the roar of the crowd. Also, he had a great sense of camaraderie with his teammates.

Much to his surprise, there were plenty of scholarships to college offered him when he graduated, and he opted for Florida State College. There he was the star of the freshman team, and his sophomore year he became All-State and All-Southern Conference halfback. Everything seemed to be coming up roses for him. He had sustained a slight knee injury, but it was on its way to healing.

Then one night he was driving along the highway when he came upon a flatbed trailer piled high with cement blocks. The trailer was slewed across the road ahead of him with no warning lights. Buddy was never one to be driving at 20 miles per hour on an open highway. He was, in fact, doing close to 90 at the time. He tried to pull his car off the road, but couldn't. He smashed into the trailer, at the last moment sliding down as far as he could in the front seat.

His instinctive reaction saved his life. But when they pulled him out of the mass of twisted steel and broken glass that had been the car, they didn't know if he was going to live or not.

His spleen was ruptured, and surgeons removed it immediately. But the bad news had to do with his knees. Both were thoroughly smashed, and the bones were set with great difficulty.

When he tried out on the football field later on, he realized that the knee injury had been aggravated so seriously that he could never be a football runner anymore. He dropped out of college.

His father was incensed at his move.

"Get back in there and fight!" he told his son. "Nobody likes a quitter. You can exercise that knee."

Buddy suddenly had enough of the tension in the

house, and the constant bickering with his authoritarian
father. He pulled up stakes this time and really left,
heading for New York City.

New York was not the city of his dreams. It was a
harsh, tough town, with streetwise hustlers and shrewd
operators of all kinds. Buddy found work at odd
jobs. He washed dishes at Schraffts. He bounced
troublemakers at Roseland Dance Hall. He did just
about every muscle job there was to do.

He wasn't alone in his own purposeless life style.
He ran into dozens of other young people who were
having trouble adjusting to society in the same way he
was. A lot of his contemporaries were trying to become
actors and artists. Buddy had about as much talent for
art as a giraffe. But he remembered he had been able to
act in high school; and he had learned how to fool his
father.

He ran into another aspiring actor named Rip
Torn, and it was Rip who actually gave Buddy the in-
centive to try out for acting. Neither of them got jobs
right away on Broadway. In fact, Buddy couldn't get
any kind of work at all, except more muscle jobs.

By 1957 he had saved up a small amount of money,
and took the train home, where he enrolled in an acting
course at Palm Beach Junior College. He got his old
bunk back at home without too much parental
displeasure and stuck it out in the school for a year.

Although he thought he wasn't getting anywhere,
he played a role in *Outward Bound* that brought him the
Florida Drama Award. That gave him the opportunity
to work professionally at the Hyde Park Playhouse in
upstate New York.

Burt was finally cast in a New York City Center
revival of *Mister Roberts*, playing Mannion. Then he
began studying acting at the Neighborhood Playhouse
with Wynn Handman.

"Wynn was wonderful," Burt recalled. "Very
gentle. It was almost impossible for me to get up in

front of people and do anything. Anything fake. And I thought acting is fake—I mean, you're acting, that's why it's called acting, isn't it?"

Television was live then, and Burt began learning how to do stunts. It was impossible to cut the camera away from an actor when the danger came, so the man who spoke the lines had to fall through the window.

"I could get up and throw someone out a window. That was real. But to get up and make believe felt foolish to me. Sometimes it still does."

At a performance in New York, actress Joanne Woodward, Paul Newman's wife, saw him and alerted her own agent to his potentialities. Music Corporation of America signed him on for a short-term deal.

Then, right after that, he was assigned a role as a guest star in an episode of *M Squad*, in which he made his television debut.

In a way, he considered himself a copout. He had tried for the stage and had settled for television. He didn't feel very happy about it, thinking of his father, who had called him a quitter for leaving college and football.

Nevertheless he soon signed a seven-year contract with Universal Pictures Television. Universal cast him as a regular in a series called *Riverboat*. He found the work stifling.

"I played Dum-Dum the whistle-blower, or something," he told an interviewer later. "I was so fed up I walked out on the series at the end of twenty-six weeks. Actually, I remember heaving the director into a lake near the set. It was a small lake. But after that I didn't have any work with Universal. Possibly there is a cause-and-effect correlation there, but I can't be sure."

He recalled: "I did some things like *Pony Express*, the kind of show they shoot with a Kodak and a flashlight. Those were depressing years."

When the acting roles dried up, he got a couple of jobs as a stunt man. Breaking his neck every other day rolling off porch roofs onto fake Western streets didn't appeal to Burt, and he decided to turn his back on Hollywood. It was his third copout. He tried not to think what his father's reaction would be.

There was always Broadway. Burt got a good break. Hugh Wheeler had just written a play called *Look: We've Come Through*. Burt won the role of Skip, a loutish sailor in the cast. It was a well-liked play—at least the critics ate it up—but not a well-received play. It closed after five performances in October, 1961.

Burt was on the bricks again.

It was television or nothing. Burt sighed and wrote his mother a letter, unable to tell his father. "Tell him I've quit again," he wrote her. "But I'm leaving New York for the West Coast."

A letter came by return mail. "Your father says the next time you come home he'll tell you how many times *he* quit—cold. 'Do what you have to do son.' That's what he told me to write you."

Burt returned to Hollywood and got jobs playing Indians and heavies on outdoor series. In 1962 he got the role of Quint Asper, the mute half-breed town blacksmith in the CBS-TV series *Gunsmoke*.

"Quite a role," he said. "I used to stare straight ahead of me and real hard at Jim Arness's belt buckle. He's six-seven, you know."

And Burt, he need not have added, was five-ten.

That same year, Burt met and married Judy Carne, an English comedienne who was the "Sock-it-to-Me" girl in the *Laugh-In* show—the one who always got water dumped on her. They were married for three years. It was a frustrating time for Burt.

Judy was gaining almost instant fame on one of *the* television shows of the year. Burt was still struggling with zero parts, like the blacksmith on *Gunsmoke*.

"It was a very heavy problem for him to have a working actress wife," Judy said.

The *Laugh-In* work was sporadic at best, and a time followed when neither of them was working. The debts piled up.

"During one of our frequent fights," Judy recalled, "I told Burt I wanted out—a divorce—and in the heat of argument he agreed. Before I knew it, we were no longer married."

The marriage was dissolved in 1965.

Burt was being touted by his agent as "another Marlon Brando." The trouble was, there was *already* one Marlon Brando, who had no intention of turning up his toes. Work was hard to get.

Finally ABC-TV jumped into the police-action race and signed Burt Reynolds as the lead in *Hawk*, a cop story about a city policeman with an Indian background. The show played during the 1966-67 season, competing each week with feature movies on another network.

Hawk scored low in the ratings, which were all-important to the network executives and the advertisers. It was cancelled after four months. Al Salerno, of the New York *World Journal Tribune* reported that after the show was cancelled, "Letters by the hundreds, including one with 250 signatures, have poured into his newspaper. It is known that the network also received substantial protest mail . . . The letter-writers raged against the network holding on to so much of what it considers pap while cutting of a strong, adult drama with a forceful central character well-acted by Burt Reynolds."

Following the demise of *Hawk*, Burt tried again in another television series. He played Dan August, a detective in a small West Coast city. *Dan August* appeared on the ABC network in the 1970-71 season, and the impact of the series was far greater than the Nielson reports showed.

It bombed, too.

By now Burt was convinced that he was playing

with a cold deck. He began to wonder if it wasn't time to get out of a business that only gave him ulcers and heartaches. But he needed money to live, and he had to act to make money. His agent got him roles, even though they weren't very good ones.

In the early 1960's—a time of upheaval in the country and a time when television and Hollywood had no idea where the entertainment industry was going—he played in such movies as *Angel Baby*, and *Armored Command* for Allied Artists in 1961; played the title role, an Indian brave, in a spaghetti Western called *Navajo Joe* for United Artists in 1967; played a featured role in several high budget films like *100 Rifles* for Twentieth Century Fox in 1969, and *Skullduggery* for Universal in 1970.

"My movies," he said, "were the kind they show in airplanes and prisons, because nobody can leave."

Reviewers liked him, and took every opportunity to play up his abilities. However, it didn't do any good with the money men in the big offices in the Manhattan penthouses.

"It's amazing," he said, "that the critics see it and the people with money don't. Someone is going to have to take a chance on me."

But not yet.

In 1968, however, the Theater Owners of America voted Burt Reynolds the "Newcomer of the Year!"

Burt got a big bang out of that accolade. "After thirteen years in the business, I'm the newcomer of the year! Those theater owners are a quick study!"

Burt had always had a caustic sense of humor. His inability to land the big role and break through the way he knew he could tended to make it even more barbed and sharp than it ordinarily would have been.

Because of this tendency to say what he thought in front of newspaper reports, interviewers, and big shots in the industry, he had got to be known as a "hostile" figure.

His agent suggested he get better exposure. Burt didn't really think exposure would help much. He figured he had already been seen by everybody—and *that* hadn't helped at all.

"Go on the talk shows," his agent ordered. "Talk. Let it all hang out."

Johnny Carson's *Tonight* show was the big insomniac talker of the era. After more nudging from his agent, Burt finally decided to go on the Carson show. And, strangely enough, it was his appearance on the talk shows that prepared him for the big breakthrough that was coming.

"I was the tight, constipated actor," he said. "I just stood there with my number three virile look and never took chances."

What kind of chances could he have taken as Quint Asper, blacksmith with sinewy muscle and stoned look? Throw an anvil at James Arness?

On the talk shows, however, Burt was a different person. He simply let it all roll out from within—the caustic comments he had always made, which had bolted the doors of success against him. However, in the unreal surroundings of the talk show—with Johnny Carson sitting there grinning and the studio people running around like crazies—Burt's acerbic wit became almost benevolent.

Besides, he had suddenly learned to stand a little off from himself and take a look at what he was and what he was doing. It was a pretty funny kind of life—a pretty dumb thing for a grown man to be doing. Standing in front of a camera and mouthing lines some shriveled-up writer had banged out on an electric typewriter and making funny faces *was* a pretty silly way to make a living.

"It's the talk shows that taught me to take chances," he said. "You just say, 'Here I am. If you don't like it, then screw you, and if you *do* like it, it's terrific.' So I thought, why don't I take those chances as an actor? Laugh at the most ridiculous things; touch somebody when I want to? *Do* it. That's what you do on a talk show. So what if you've been working ten years making a nice living, why don't you start taking chances?"

And so he was no longer the "constipated actor." In fact, the quick easy wit he had always had flowed much more freely in front of millions of viewers. People who were potential motion picture and television fans got to know him as a fun person. He got natural exposure as Burt Reynolds, real guy.

"The talk shows changed everything drastically overnight," he said. "Suddenly I had a personality. People had heard of me."

Now he could be more relaxed with the print media writers, kidding himself unmercifully.

"I have short legs," he told one writer. "Someone else is walking around with my legs. If I had the legs I'm supposed to have. I would be six feet five inches—a *big* actor!"

He could kid about his womanizing. His philosophy of life, he told a reporter, was basically simple. "I fool around, I chase girls, I chase life, I pick up all the options. That's what it's all about, isn't it?"

He got a big charge out of his image in the movie capital. "Around Hollywood," he said, "I'm thought of as redneck heaven."

He had a red-painted farmhouse-style hideaway right near the Sunset Strip. It had rooms with red walls and red cushions. "Red makes me feel good," he told a friend.

"It's really gauche," he described his home once. "It's my movie star house."

He drove a red sports car with a white top and white leather seats, and a license plate specially numbered for him: "EGO 22."

"I thought twenty-two sounded like an enormous amount of ego," he said. "Besides, two's have always been good for me. I was the second son, born in the second month, the eleventh day—that adds up to two—my football number in college was twenty-two.''

He cracked jokes about his career. "You should meet my father. He loves television, watches everything on it. Except me. When I come on the screen, he leaves the room.''

More about his father: "It's an Old Southern idea that no man is a man until his father tells him he is. My Old Man hasn't given me the word yet.''

He loved his father, too. "When he comes into the room, he fills the doorway,'' Burt said in awe.

Three things happened almost simultaneously in 1971 to bring Burt Reynolds out into the open and thrust him straight up to the top as the most identifiable male of the time.

One was his appearance as the first nude male centerfold in history. The second was his appearance in the motion picture *Deliverance*.

And the third was his appearance on the Dinah Shore show as a guest, which led to one of the most talked-about love affairs in entertainment history.

To take the third happening first, it was Dinah who became his confidante and guide through the period in which he leaped into national prominence.

"She had written me to be on her show,'' Burt recalled, "and after three or four months I finally did go on.''

He had been on talk shows before, but when he faced Dinah, suddenly he was not himself.

"I said terrible, unexpected things,'' he confessed. "I said, 'I want to talk to you about going to Palm Springs with me for the weekend.' It was hard for her to cope with me—she was making a stew at the time.''

It took the technicians two hours of taping to get a fifteen-minute segment for the show, because "one hour and forty-five minutes of the conversation was X-rated,'' as Dinah put it.

"I liked her mind," Burt said later. "I fell in *like*."

The upshot of the show was that Dinah *did* go to Palm Springs with Burt. In this easygoing fashion started the big Burt Reynolds/Dinah Shore love affair. What added piquancy to the relationship was the fact that it did not wind up in marriage at all.

"She's a special lady. Lady with a capital 'L.' And that's the best thing you could say about her," Burt said of Dinah.

To a reporter, he gave this accolade:

"There are only two men in Hollywood who never have anything bad to say about anybody. One of them is Carol Burnett. But she's married with a lot of kids. The other is Dinah, and she was free."

Dinah was as outspoken about Burt as he was about her.

"We met on my show," she said. "When people ask how we got together, I laugh and say, 'We are computer mated.' I had seen Burt before, of course, on the Merv Griffin show and other talk shows, and I had been attracted to him at once, even though we hadn't actually met.

"When he came on the show I liked him still more. First of all, and obviously, he was a dreamboat. Second, I was pleased to see he had a genuine sense of fun. After that we met again and finally we began to go steady.

"I think what binds us together is that we both have a fear and dislike of quarrels. He's Aquarius, I'm Pisces, which means that we just have to live our lives harmoniously, everything else is intolerable.

"We laugh together, which relaxes me. If he'd been the type of man who likes powerful confrontations, strong discussions, endless arguments, we couldn't possibly have gotten along."

Pisces and Aquarius sailed on into a rare brilliance of exposure that became grist for the newspaper mills, judging from the vast amount of newsprint used up in publicizing the romance.

When Dinah said that she and Burt were computer-mated, she was joking, but the truth was not really very far from that. Psychologists have always known that certain people tend to select a look-alike mate, even the second and third times around. In effect, Dinah was still looking for George again.

A columnist noted that George Montgomery and Burt Reynolds were in no way dissimilar. In fact, he said, if you took a photograph of George Montgomery and put a thick mustache on it, you would come up with a non-existent person who looked exactly like Burt Reynolds.

The truth was that there were many more similarities between the two men than dissimilarities.

Item: George Montgomery spent his youth as a cowboy, working on a ranch in Montana where he was born. Burt Reynolds was born near a ranch, and his father worked as a cowboy.

Item: They were both born in cattle country, even though at almost opposite ends of the country.

Item: George Montgomery broke into the movies through doing stunt work as a rider. Burt Reynolds went into stunt work when his ongoing career as an actor sputtered and almost went out.

Item: Both men were tall and strong, with excellent physiques, and projected virility and masculinity without effort.

Item: Both men were magnetic people who drew women to them so easily they almost had to fight them off with clubs.

And, of course, the most obvious similarity of all: Both men had fallen in love with the same woman, Dinah Shore, who, reciprocally, had fallen in love with them.

Dinah never apparently noticed the interesting comparison, or, if she did, never commented on it. Nor did Burt.

Actually, he was becoming increasingly annoyed at

the way the gossip columnists treated him and
Dinah—particularly Dinah.

"The press chastised her, killed her, and didn't say
very nice things about me for a long, long time when we
first got together.

"Then they finally said, 'Well, what the hell,
they're just *perfect* for each other.' "

Burt recalled one interview which served as an
example of the kind of thing both of them were subjected to.

"This guy calls up and says he's from the Boston
Something-or-other. I meet him, and he's Mister
Warmth. I notice he isn't taking any notes. 'You like
older women, don't you?' he asks me. 'Wouldn't you
say you like women who have it all together?'

'I notice he's finishing sentences for me. I finally
wring it out of him that he isn't a Boston newspaper
reporter at all, he's from the *National Enquirer*! The
son of a bitch, seven years ago I would have taken his
head off and spit in it. 'Why did you lie?' I asked him.

"He was trying to get a story about a lady that
nobody in the world has ever been able to say a bad
thing about. Whether Dinah's older than I am, or I'm
older than she is, what difference does it make? The
things she's learned in life, I'm the guy who gets to reap
all those rewards. And if it runs its course some day, I'll
run with it until it runs out . . . and she'll be richer for it,
and I'll be richer for it."

Early in 1972 Helen Gurley Brown, the editor of
Cosmopolitan, told Burt Reynolds that the magazine intended to run a gag photograph in the centerfold.

"It's going to be a putdown of *Playboy*," she explained to him. "Instead of a nude woman, we're going
to feature a nude man."

"Oh," said Burt. "Who is it going to be?"

"You."

Burt thought it over, wondering just how it was
going to affect his floundering motion picture career

and his relationship with Dinah Shore.

He told Dinah about it. And, according to him, she saw the humor of the controversial centerfold picture right away.

"I'll tell you, if she had thought it was awful, I'd have thought twice about going through with it," Burt said.

Dinah didn't recall it quite that way.

"I feel there are certain things that are treasurable," she said, "and my heart and my soul and my body are very important to me. I'm basically shy and withdrawn, and I can't stand exhibitionism. It's totally against my nature.

"Explicit portrayals of sex bother me terribly because they take all the loveliness out of everything, rip aside all our illusions. God, the illusions are important—to be able to imagine. I don't live *in* the illusion. I enjoy sex, but I'm not a voyeur. I should think a stag movie would be the turn-off of all time—a turn-off of life."

So when Burt told her about the nude centerfold *Cosmopolitan* wanted him to do, Dinah was shocked.

"I thought it was *very* bad idea," she said. "Bad for his image, *worse* for mine!"

She told him how she felt, but confessed later that perhaps she had not expressed herself forcefully enough. "That's always been one of my problems."

According to her version, she told him: "No, no, no, don't do it. It's a crazy idea."

He replied: "It's a first. I think it'll work."

Dinah insisted. "No, I don't want it."

But he had already made up his mind. "It's going to be funny."

Burt went ahead and made the picture.

"You can say I was overridden," she said.

With a great deal of trepidation, Dinah waited for the proofs of the photograph, feeling "pretty darned awful."

"That day he brought them home, I was afraid to look at them. Then, when I finally saw them, I had to laugh. I just fell over! I realized the whole thing wasn't at all distasteful. It was simply the biggest put-on of all time."

But the centerfold helped skyrocket Burt Reynolds into national prominence. The April, 1972, *Cosmopolitan* walked off the stands, as industry distributors said. Over 700,000 extra copies of that issue of *Cosmopolitan* were sold. The centerfold was reprinted in one of the news magazines later on, with a big story about him.

Eyebrows were lifted, gossip columnists gleefully invented a new word, "beef-cake," to describe male "cheese-cake," editorialists worried about the morals of children who might see the picture, and adults, too. No one was unaffected.

"I don't believe children are turned on by it," scoffed Burt. "They can see more in a Sears Roebuck catalogue. When I list the three most unimportant events in my life, this will be one of them!"

Kay Gardella was interested in Dinah's reaction to the picture, and asked Burt about it during an interview.

"Dinah is a classy dame," he answered, "with a greal deal of taste. I have a lot of respect for her. I would not have jumped into the deal unless she said it was okay. Fortunately, she has a sense of humor and so does the public. I'm glad to see that most people took it in the way it was intended—as a put-on."

No matter how many times he repeated that, it didn't get through to everybody. It still turned on a lot of girls who otherwise might have ignored him. "Women will rush across a room at a cocktail party now just to say they don't find me attractive," he grinned.

According to Dinah, the repercussions from the centerfold continued for a long time afterward.

"Much later," she said, "some friends came back

from Tijuana and they brought us a copy of the centerfold in the form of a painting on velvet. It was six feet long and horribly life-size. Crazy!"

Dinah became philosophical about the furor after awhile. "Actually, I feel it's helped, not so much because of the publicity, but because it's all so very amusing, and because the image we both want for him is as a funny man."

Not too much later and certainly before the furor about the centerfold had died down, Warner Brothers released the motion picture *Deliverance*, directed by John Boorman. The picture was a film version of James Dickey's action novel about four Atlanta businessmen who spend a weekend on a canoe trip through the Georgia mountains.

Burt played the part of Lewis Medlock, the leader of the quartet. The role called for a very "macho" he-man whose manhood and philosophy of life were tested by the wilds and the people he was with. The role was strong; Burt's portrayal was strong.

One critic called his performance "tough and powerful." *A Time* writer said: "The movie was Reynolds' own deliverance. Overnight he became the Frog Prince of Hollywood."

There was, however, a slight problem with the unfortunate juxtaposition of the centerfold, a put-on, and the strong role in *Deliverance*, a serious professional effort. The public did not really know how to take Burt now—as the humorous man they watched on television and saw clowning in *Cosmo*, or the serious man they saw in *Deliverance*.

"It was too bad the two things happened so close together," Burt later lamented.

But from those months on, Burt Reynolds was a *personality*. And his ongoing affair with Dinah Shore certainly kept things hot on the front burner.

Reporters were constantly at each of them to comment on their feelings for one another. In exasperation,

Burt once told a tenacious reporter:

"The relationship is very very good. With a capital V, capital V, capital G. The relationship has never been as the movie magazines say, *that serious*. Nor that far apart. I like to be with her. And if somebody said that tonight Mars and Venus are going to collide, I'd go over to share it with her."

Another aggressive reporter cornered Dinah, and the dialogue went like this:

"Dinah, you sound like an extremely happy woman."

"I am."

"You are in love."

"What sort of question is that? In fact, is it a question?"

"It isn't a question. It's an observation."

"Well, okay. I accept your observation."

"Then I am talking to a woman in love?"

"Yes," she said.

And one writer bore down on Burt to find out his thoughts about marriage.

"I believe in good marriages," said Burt, dead pan. "I also believe in the Tooth Fairy." Then he shook his head. "I couldn't ever go through another marriage. That would just wreck me. The first one almost destroyed me." He was talking about his life with Judy Carne. "Divorce takes too much out of you.

"At this particular time, I'm not sure what marriage would do to my so-called image—or, for that matter, what my image would do to marriage."

But Dinah was answering questions about marriage in a slightly different fashion. Asked if she would ever marry again, she said: "I think so, under the right circumstances. It's a waste of life if you don't. Marriage is the ultimate way to whatever fulfillment you want, but it is something that one wants to work out very carefully."

Later, to another interviewer, she said, "I don't

want to marry Burt. Why spoil a good thing?'' And she added: ''Everything is fine and comfortable and easy and nice.''

And Burt soon got into print discussing ''older'' women. ''At thirty-four or thirty-five, a woman knows who she is and doesn't play games. There's something twice as attractive about that. A nineteen-year-old not playing games doesn't know what games she's not playing.''

By the end of the year, everyone in the country was talking about ''the affair.''

In November, 1971, Irv Kupcinet, the columnist, commented, ''If you caught Burt Reynolds on Dinah Shore's TV show the other A.M., you know their romance is steady as you go. They were as giddy as two moonstruck teenagers.''

In December, Earl Wilson had a go at it, too:

''Dinah Shore is more vivacious, scintillating and attractive and all those other adjectives than she's been in years, undoubtedly due to her friendship with Burt Reynolds, according to all her Hollywood girlfriends, who go so far as to say that when seeing them together one thinks only of her youthful appearance.''

Even the camera crew of her television show were quoted by the print medium: ''She's very much in love with him,'' one said. Another added: ''She's ecstatic every time he's around the studio. She becomes a different person.''

Somebody even squeezed a comment out of Charles Pomerantz, her press agent in Hollywood. ''It's true that she's dated no one else since she met Burt Reynolds,'' he said. ''She says Burt is very attractive and very masculine, with a great sense of humor. She obviously enjoys herself immensely with him.''

11

No Promises

Meanwhile, the affair was moving right along even in the bright glare of publicity. Dinah traveled East with Burt to his home in Florida. With his movie money Burt had bought a big 180-acre ranch near the town of Jupiter that had once belonged to gangster Al Capone. On it he raised horses and Angus beef cattle.

They spent their time riding horses and Honda motorcycles. When Dinah took a bad spill on a two-wheeled bike, she got a mouthful of sand and crushed seashells. Burt then made a gallant gesture, and bought her a present of a three-wheeled, balloon-tired model. He even hired a contractor to build a tennis court for Dinah to play on. Tennis wasn't Burt's game at all, but he played when she wanted him to.

"I've always wanted a jock for a love," he told a friend one day.

Burt's house was actually the showplace of the ranch. It was built on a concrete column in the middle of a lake.

The happy pair motored down to West Palm Beach to see Burt's parents. Then they went over to visit the family clergyman, Dr. Jess C. Moody, senior minister of the First Baptist Church of West Palm Beach.

"They attended my church together and spoke with me in my office afterward," Dr. Moody said. "Two days before, my wife and I went to Burt's home in Jupiter. It's a typical bachelor's pad, and a terrific place." Dr. Moody added: "I didn't ask them if they were in love, but there is too much smoke for there not to be a fire."

By now the affair was the talk of the entertainment world. Judy Carne, Burt's ex-wife, described the romance between her ex-husband and Dinah as "strange and weird. Frankly, I think the whole relationship is a bit of a hideaway from people for Burt.

"He feels it'll keep the ladies away if he has a heavy relationship going. I can't see him marrying the lady because he wants children very much."

George Montgomery, Dinah's ex, had something to say about Dinah and Burt, too. "I think Dinah's romance with Burt is marvelous and great. I'm happy she's found love with a wonderful man," said Montgomery. "If Burt makes her happy, then I'm happy for her. I've never met Reynolds. He's a hell of an actor and I think he did a great job in *Deliverance*.

"Dinah can make men very comfortable," he said. "She's still vivacious and youthful looking. She's a very intelligent, warm, fun-loving woman. I see her from time to time but she hasn't confided in me about any marriage plans."

Because of Dinah and Burt, *Playgirl* asked Montgomery to pose for a nude centerfold. He turned them down. "I'm doing commercials for a company whose officials said the publicity would destroy my television image."

Meanwhile Burt's career was booming. He did a good job in Woody Allen's comic movie, *Everything You Always Wanted to Know About Sex But Were Afraid to Ask*, for United Artists in 1972. He starred as an inept policeman in the movie version of Ed McBain's 87th Precinct Novel *Fuzz*, also for United Artists. The next year he played the title role of a Brooklyn private detective in *Shamus*, for Columbia. "It's a bang-up exciter of a picture and Burt Reynolds gives it an extra dimension for force and dry humorous charm," wrote one critic.

He then signed with M-G-M. to play the lead opposite Sarah Miles, a British actress, in *The Man Who Loved Cat Dancing*. The story was based on a best-selling period novel by Marilyn Durham about a high-born lady who found her true love in a Western desperado named Joy Grobart. Grobart was a widower of Shoshone squaw Cat Dancing, hence the trick title. Burt played Grobart, who had turned to train robbing as a method of obtaining money to ransom his children from the tribe that had custody of them.

In February the picture was being shot on location in Gila Bend, Arizona. Sarah's business agent, a young man named David Whiting, was accompanying her during the shooting. Younger than Sarah, who was married to producer Robert Bolt, Whiting was a star-struck personality with a Bond Street wardrobe, lavender glasses, and a lust for the life of "the Beautiful People."

He had once dated starlet Inger Stevens, who had committed suicide in 1970, and then had a crush on Candice Bergen. In the words of some, he was "half mad." At one time a Hollywood correspondent for *Time* magazine, he was described by the Luce gang as "at least flaky." He had ups and downs. During rages he fought and during depressions he made "at least one suicide attempt," according to Sarah.

On the night of February 10, after the day's shooting was over, the cast retired to the Palomino Bar and Restaurant in Ajo, a community near Gila Bend, to attend a party for visiting talk-show host Merv Griffin. Sarah went with Burt Reynolds, but got bored when the party turned out to be a supper party rather than a cocktail party.

Lee J. Cobb drove her home in his Maserati-powered Citroen. At his digs they spent several hours drinking and talking. Then Sarah knocked on Burt's door to find him with his Japanese masseuse. Sarah apologized for walking out on him in Ajo, and then went back to her own motel at about three A.M.

Whiting was there, angry and roaring drunk. "Where have you been?" he demanded, repeating the phrase at least three times.

"None of your business," snapped Sarah.

"If you don't tell me, I'll kill you!" he screamed.

She turned her back on him. He started slamming her around. She refused to fight back. Attracted by the row, Jane Evans, the governess of Sarah's five-year-old, ran in. She found Sarah on the floor and Whiting astride her, slapping her.

"Get Burt!" yelled Sarah.

Jane got Burt. He came running over. By then Whiting was up and Sarah was rubbing her bruised body.

"If I was not as mature as I am now, I would have laid him out," Burt said later.

He simply grabbed Sarah and told her she could stay at his place for the night. She went out with him, leaving Whiting there, white-faced and glowering.

In the morning Sarah went back to her room and found Whiting dead in the bathroom, clutching an empty pill container, with methaqualone pills scattered all over the floor. He had apparently taken an overdose of the pills.

Sarah ran over to Burt's. He came back immediately.

"I guess I saw it in a movie," Burt said later. "But I leaned over and felt his pulse." Whiting's hand was ice-cold. He was dead. "I took the pill container out of his hand, like a dummy." Burt related. Then, he said, he must have lost it.

The company closed down the set while the Arizona authorities investigated the death of Whiting. There were some unexplained injuries on Whiting's body—one an inch-wide star-shaped gash on the back of his head. There were enough gaps in the story to necessitate a more extended investigation.

The M-G-M. attorneys tried to confine Sarah and Burt to written statements about what had happened, but the judge eventually decided that they must appear in court. They did so. And of course the story was by now a juicy front-page scandal, with Burt's name linked with Sarah's in most of the world's newspapers.

Dinah was in Hollywood when she heard about the crisis at Gila Bend. She flew out to do what she could to help Burt through the turmoil and tension of the investigation. After he had been questioned by the authorities, she shared a motor home with him, and then they finally retired to Wayne Newton's ranch in Las Vegas.

What made the David Whiting death so weird and hair-raising for Burt was the fact that Inger Stevens, who had once dated David Whiting, had also dated Burt Reynolds at the time of her suicide.

Dinah's strong personal support got Burt through the messy, messy weeks that followed. Eventually the autopsy found that Whiting had died of an overdose of methaqualone, but the case was left open on the books.

There were other pressures as well for Burt. He

began blowing his top or snapping out smart answers to newsmen when he should have been polite and cool. On the other hand, he frequently made the perfect rejoinder to exasperating questions about marriage to Dinah.

Barbara Walters, who was living apart from her husband at the time, kept needling Burt on the *Today Show* in July, 1973 about his relationship with Dinah. She finally got him to admit he was in love with her.

"Well, if you love her," she said, "why don't you get married?"

"Why don't you get divorced?" Burt responded.

Generally, he pointed out to interviewers that his relationship with Dinah Shore was not something to laugh about at all. "It's too precious a relationship. It's easy for me to be flippant about my career, but not about this. There are too many relationships that become public property because people don't take care of them. As for marriage, well, I think if we were going to be married, we would be."

About that time Dinah made a comment to the effect that she didn't particularly want to be married to Burt. "I don't want to grow old in his arms," she said with a smile.

"She really is the best female friend I have," Burt pointed out, "maybe *the* best friend."

Meanwhile, Dinah's television career as a talk-show hostess was going along at a fine clip. In all her years of show business, she had never once been fired from a job. She had withdrawn from programs, and she had finished up seasons that were never intended to be renewed, and she had failed to get jobs—but she never had been "terminated"—as the entertainment brass always puts it.

That is, up until May, 1974.

In that month *Dinah's Place* won an Emmy Award for the best daytime talk-variety show, and she, as hostess, was to pick up the Emmy for being the best hostess in talk, service, or variety.

The NBC Vice-President of Networks sent her a wire to tell her the good news.

"Congratulations on winning another Emmy Award for the early morning Dinah Shore Show," the wire began.

After the good news came the bad news.

"I'm sorry the exigencies of business require us to drop your show," the telegram continued. "We hope we can work together again." And it was signed, "Larry White, Network Vice President."

Dinah reacted in character. "I really thought it was a gag," she said. She laughed and immediately sent a response to White.

"I just got the funniest wire. It said my award-winning show was cancelled. Some dummy signed your name to it."

Later a telephone call came in for Dinah. It was Larry White. "It's no joke," he told her. "It's true."

Dinah had been working for NBC for 26 years, ever since her first appearance on radio in 1938. She simply could not believe it.

"It was a terrible, terrible experience," she said. "The ratings on 'Dinah's Place' were way up there. We were the only show on the network that had a waiting list of sponsors."

Speculation among her associates for the rationale of the cancellation was that the Dinah Shore show had the misfortune of being slotted between two so-called "game shows." The NBC philosophy current at the time held with "block booking." Dinah's talk show broke the game-show block and hence had to go.

Whatever the reason, Dinah was out. The last *Dinah's Place* was taped for July 19, 1974. And she was briefly but deeply shaken up over the decision by her network to drop her after all those years.

Never a lady to wallow in the slough of despond for long, Dinah shrugged off her depression within three days, sat down with Henry Jaffe, and dreamed up a new talk show format to peddle to the opposition.

CBS loved it and they bought it.

"CBS even allowed me to be a little more controversial, something NBC never allowed me to be," she said.

The show as retitled *Dinah!* and started up October 21.

At first *Dinah!* was televised on the five CBS-owned television stations across the country on a "best-bid" basis. But as the show got going and the ratings began moving up, almost every major market in the United States soon acquired it. Meanwhile, back at the NBC ranch, ulcers were the order of the day. Two Excedrins and a glass of water became known as the "NBC Blue Plate Special" in the executive dining room. And soon Larry White—actually programming chief although his title was Network Vice-President—vanished from NBC.

The new Dinah Shore show prospered.

Variety bought it right off the bat. "Dinah Shore's new 90-minute variety-entertainment daily strip got itself launched in quite acceptable form on Monday, if such a judgment can be made for the edited hour, the version that is being aired by CBS-TV's New York flagship," the paper said.

"The Shore warmth is an expected, acknowledged asset of the series and the content fits the early morning hour quite well." *Variety* even predicted that the show would quickly establish itself as "sold competition to Mike [Douglas] and Merv [Griffin]."

Bob Goodman, television critic of the Atlanta *Journal*, wrote a solid appreciation of her. "Miss Shore was considered ready to join the 'over the hill' gang a decade or so ago when she finally gave up her nighttime weekly series. She had all the money she needed and it was felt that she would join the 'leisure class' of Beverly Hills, working only when and if she wanted to, playing tennis with big-name celebrities the rest of the time.

"Nothing could be more distant from the truth, at least as far as the 'leisure' bit is concerned. She and NBC came up with the *Dinah Shore Show* format and this daytime series ran for several seasons, usually winning an Emmy or two each time the awards were distributed.

"Her visibility on television kept her on the public's mind and her highly publicized romance with a much-younger Burt Reynolds proved to everyone that she was not ready for an 'old folks' home.' "

He went on, "I have met and talked with Miss Shore on numerous occasions over the years, and in case you are wondering if, perhaps, she is 'different' offstage than she is 'on,' you can forget it. A more personable and easy-going lady, one who exudes more charm and 'class' you will never find.

"I am unabashedly a Dinah Shore fan."

Randy Sue Coburn, of the Washington *Star*, wrote, "Now that the car-hustling voice of TV's golden years is getting wobbly, her belle-ish Tennessee upbringing continues to serve her well."

When Walter Cronkite had appeared on her show some years before, she wrote, he told Dinah that he had never been interviewed better or seen anyone who had done his or her homework more thoroughly than she did.

The beautiful thing about the show, another Washington critic wrote, was that she exhibited "absolute zero instinct for the jugular." It meant, generally, "pure, congenial entertainment" for the viewer.

"[That attitude] books people like Spiro Agnew to her show," the critic went on. "And brings people like Eugene McCarthy by her table at Sans Souci [in Washington] to say a congenial hello."

Dinah had always understood the velvet approach. "I don't back people into a corner," she said. "Barbara [Walters] is so good at that."

When she had Sprio Agnew on the show some time

after he had resigned the vice-presidency, she discussed
his book, *The Canfield Decision*. Before the interview
started, they agreed on ground rules insisted on by
Agnew. He would not talk about his resignation or
about Richard Nixon. Dinah complied congenially.

"I think the interview came off in a very interesting
way," she said. "I couldn't act like nothing had ever
happened, so we talked about his bitterness. I'm no
reporter, but when you have a controversial figure on,
you have an obligation to inform people."

"Of all the television talk show hosts and
hostesses," Frank Getlein wrote, "she is by far the
pleasantest to watch. Her friendly interest in her guests,
her just plain niceness, are a refreshing contrast to the
raucous aggression more typical of the species.

"You have to play a lot of heads-up ball before you
can be as successfully relaxed as she is now."

But it wasn't all work and no play for Dinah. She
still kept up with her Number Two hobby—cooking.
Craig Claiborne of *The New York Times* came out to
visit her and sample her fare.

"When Dinah invited us to dine in her home," he
wrote, "we accepted with unusual alacrity. In addition
to being a well-known singer, she is justly celebrated as
one of the finest cooks in Beverly Hills, and to be corny
as Kansas, we have long wanted to be 'someone in the
kitchen with Dinah,' no matter how briefly. To tell the
truth, we are a bit jealous of Burt Reynolds."

He was quite taken with Dinah's *cioppino,* a
kind of seafood mix. The name is Italian dialect for
"chopped," apparently, although no one really knows.
It contains chopped rock cod, red snapper and/or sea
bass cut up in little bite-size pieces.

The gourmet writer saluted Dinah as an "intuitive
cook," meaning she was a natural-born expert in
cookery. And Dinah liked to dine like a gourmet, occasionally sneaking out to eat at Bryan's, a place that
specialized in pit-barbecued pork, and at Patsy

d'Amore's, celebrated for its California-style pizza. But she continued to entertain small gatherings of her best friends at home.

One change was made in the *Dinah!* show the next year. CBS executives, agonizing as always over the schedule, made an in-depth study of demographics, consumer reaction, viewing proclivities of the U.S. viewer, and huddled long and grimly over the Dinah Shore show.

When the dust had settled, a directive came down to rename the show—to *Dinah* (without the exclamation point).

A satisfactory explanation as to why the change had been made never was forthcoming.

The show continued to prosper. In fact, in the summer of 1976, a summer series called *Dinah and Her New Best Friends* was developed, featuring young fledgling performers.

In 1976 Dinah was named "Entertainer of the Year" by the Conference of Personal Managers at their Twentieth Annual Award Dinner at the Crystal Room of the Beverly Hills Hotel. Four hundred guests were there.

She was, in *Variety's* quippy style, "first femme ever to receive org's award." Her talent was "kudosed" by Dennis C. Stanfill, an executive involved in the syndication of her show. Then Dinah did a comedy routine about a personal manager trying to explain what a personal manager is to his mother.

"Dinah got a big mitt" for this, said *Variety.*

And, meanwhile, what about "Big B"? (Burt Reynolds referred familiarly to Dinah as "Big D.")

By 1975 the much-ogled pair were having an increasing number of lovers' tiffs. On one occasion Burt complained to Dinah about her working hours. Burt never saw her until she got home at ten o'clock or later. Dinah rearranged her taping schedule, turning the studio upside down.

"Believe me," said Dinah, "when Burt's not happy —I'm not happy. So I don't come home late anymore. We turned our whole schedule around at the studio, and I'm through by 6:30 now. That means that Burt is happier and I'm happier."

It seemed that there was more to the deterioration of their relationship than the fact that Dinah got home late. Something was definitely amiss. The well-publicized affair had now been going on for almost four years. The two were seen everywhere together, neither one dating anyone else.

And then suddenly everything went poof.

What broke up the romance no one ever knew. But suddenly it was all over.

Early in 1975 Burt took off for location shooting in Guaymas, Mexico, where he was making a motion picture called *Lucky Lady*. Dinah flew down for weekends when Burt wasn't working.

"She really lit up the place," a member of the movie company said. "She seemed to be very happy to be around Burt." Everything went along quite smoothly, he said.

Dinah even flew home Sunday nights on the movie company charter plane with Burt's dirty laundry.

Then, quite suddenly, and without any warning, a notice appeared in Joyce Haber's Hollywood gossip column on April 19 to the effect that Burt had called it quits with Dinah. The press copied the Haber item and it was soon all over everywhere.

Dinah's friends—and they were, as always, legion —rallied to her cause. Farrah Fawcett-Majors—Mrs. Lee Majors, later to become *the* angel in television's *Charlie's Angels*—blamed Burt in print and said he had "leaked" the news to the columnist through his press agent because he was afraid to inform Dinah it was all over. "He just didn't have the guts to tell her to her face!" she said.

David Gershenson, Burt's press agent, denied in print that he had leaked rumors of the split to the press, and said he'd take a lie detector test to prove it. No one seemed to have one handy.

In addition, he implied that the whole thing was a tempest in a teapot, and not really worth talking about.

"Burt feels he and Dinah were never married," he pointed out, "so he doesn't understand the big deal. Burt doesn't feel he has to justify ending the relationship. It's as if they were just going together—dating—and they stopped."

Jane Brolin, wife of *Marcus Welby* star Jim Brolin, said, "The breakup is awfully hard on Dinah. She gives everything she has to her man. She gives and gives and gives. I don't know how she'll keep going on, but she will."

Another friend, Wayne Rogers of *M*A*S*H,* said, "I just can't bring myself to tell you what she said and how she acted. People say Burt Reynolds is a nice guy . . . but . . ."

Peter Marshall, of TV's *Hollywood Squares,* said, "Dinah puts on a good front, smiling and looking pretty. You can tell she's terribly upset only if you know her. Some people feel that Dinah will never get another man because she's an older woman."

Dinah had been completely in the dark about the breakup, even after news of it appeared in the papers. She actually thought she hadn't heard from Burt in Mexico that week because the telephone circuits were busy. However, once a few days had passed, she knew that something was wrong.

When she read the notice in the newspaper, she was tempted to laugh it off, just the way she had laughed off Larry White's telegram about the cancellation of her television show on NBC. "I won't believe it until I hear it from Burt," she told her friends.

But when she didn't get her usual invitation to join

the charter group for the weekend plane trip, she knew the report was probably right. But she wouldn't see the press.

"She's not saying anything," Farrah said, acting as her spokesperson. "She's just crying."

The breakup was a mess. It was bound to be. The "perfect May-December affair" couldn't end without embarrassment to somebody.

Reporters finally found Burt on location in Mexico but couldn't get anything out of him, either. He only admitted he was having problems with his personal life. He gave no details about what had really happened. But there were no more weekend jaunts for Dinah, no more laundry runs to Guaymas.

Dinah was down in the dumps for months. Then quite suddenly, in October, Burt sent her a warm personal letter along with some flowers. He told her he would meet her wherever she wanted, that he was coming back for good.

She signed a lease for a $300,000 beach house in Malibu. When Burt came back, the two of them moved in. They began going out together, dining at intimate spots like "The Saloon" in Beverly Hills, and it was like old times.

"We are friends again," Burt told everybody. "It's untrue to say there's a romance—but Dinah is my very best friend."

Dinah immediately made plans to redecorate her Beverly Hills home. To her friends that meant that she was in a good mood once again. People could talk to her about Burt. When the romance was on the fritz, no one could mention his name around her.

Soon Burt flew down to Valdosta, Georgia, where he began shooting a new movie, *Gator*. The press moved in on him.

"Sure, I intend to see Dinah often," he told them. "I've been to her place at Malibu, and I'll see her again whenever we've got things to talk about."

Although she was almost her old self again. Dinah's friends noticed that she was not completely recovered from the low she had experienced when Burt was off in Mexico.

"Dinah's in a kind of limbo right now," one explained. "She still loves Burt and I think that deep down she's afraid to admit the romance is over."

Taking advantage of the rumored breakup, several Hollywood stars began making tentative passes at Dinah. She turned them all down. Two of them were actors and friends of Burt's.

"They both know how much Burt and I mean to each other, and now they want to get in on the action," Dinah complained.

The waiting game paid off for Dinah. In December, Burt was once again living in Dinah's Beverly Hills home.

The "best friends" cliché seemed abrogated, the romance flowering more sweetly than ever.

"It's even more beautiful now," Burt told a reporter. "We're back together, and it's lovely."

To prove the viability of the romance, the two of them pooled their money to invest jointly in a big Los Angeles condominium project.

Burt got it all off his chest one night to a friend.

"I almost went off my rocker in Mexico because I missed her," Burt said. "And I was working under terrible conditions. It was the most grueling film I've ever made—not made any easier by the fact that deep down I wanted to be somewhere else with Dinah."

It was the same as it always had been—and yet it *wasn't* the same as it always had been. In romance, there is no going back.

Burt put it this way. "I feel exactly the same way I've always felt: She is the best friend I have in the whole word, and I will always love her. The relationship has never been like Lombard and Gable all the time. There were times when it was. But in terms of her being my best friend, we're closer now than we ever were. But I'm not only seeing her, and she's not only seeing me.''

He meant that each of them was dating others too.

He tried to analyze his feelings for Dinah after the breakup. "Once you get past the fireworks stage, it's really difficult to pass on to the next stage gracefully, and then on to the next stage. I was in the third stage of that rocket with Dinah, and it was really pleasant and terrific. It's just that I was in that third stage too early. I wasn't ready for it.''

He shook his head. "I want to have a couple of more first stages with some other people, I guess. And I agree with everybody who would say that's a very selfish person who does that. I've never admitted to being anything else.''

As for Dinah, she refused to talk about Burt to anyone. One reporter wrote, "No, Burt hasn't dumped Dinah. He still takes her out, but remember, he has never had the reputation of being a one-woman man. Dinah won't comment, and, as a matter of fact, refuses to give interviews unless the reporter agrees ahead of time not to ask about Burt.''

But she did in fact begin dating other men: Ron Ely, one-time Tarzan star on television; Iggy Pop, far-out rock star; and Joe Iacovetta, former pro tennis star. With Dinah, actions always spoke louder than words, anyway.

She had survived other disappointments—other catastrophes, actually—and she would survive this one.

For example, nothing could have been worse for a budding starlet than the collapse of her screen career in the 1950's. Yet she almost immediately moved on into television, and became its reigning queen.

Her two marriages had both ended in disaster—and yet she had survived to become the love object of one of the motion picture screen's most romantic and macho characters, Burt Reynolds.

That highly publicized Reynolds affair, one television critic wrote, "did much to encourage the now popular idea that age has little to do with a fine life."

Burt, in fact, had put his finger on Dinah's amazing durability when he said, "She has the body of a 25-year-old with the mind of a cultured, mature woman."

And even after the Dinah-Burt affair ended, she was still in excellent physical, psychological, and mental health—and is to this day.

"After more than three decades in show business, Dinah Shore—singer, actress and talk-show hostess—is still in full bloom," one magazine writer observed. "She exudes a sense of well-being," she wrote, "her skin enviably fresh and taut, her 123 pounds firmly and compactly displayed on her 5 foot 6 inch frame."

The mystery of Dinah's staying power is something that has baffled even her. But she once expressed herself on the subject by mentioning several possible causes for it.

"Not being pretty really helped. I never sat back and said, 'Look, I'm pretty.' Nobody ever said I was. So I always worked on my appearance."

It took her awhile, she points out, to learn that too much makeup, especially a lot of powder, was something that might make her age rapidly. And so she stayed away from it.

But she cites a number of other reasons for her durability.

"I love to exercise," she admits. "Tennis, swimming, and I really love golf." She still spends her weekends playing doubles with friends, and for a really hard workout, she plays with a tennis pro.

"I don't have a weight problem because I don't take seconds." When her weight starts edging up over the 125-pound mark, she senses that she may be approaching trouble, and she starts eating smaller portions.

Working is one of her most effective means of controlling her weight.

"I work hard and when I'm not working hard, I'm either lying around or playing golf or tennis." The sport itself matters to her, not winning the game." It would be nice to win more often than lose, but it's not absolutely essential," she says. "What is essential is that it be comfortable and fun. The outdoor-indoor life in Southern California makes it come out that way for me."

As for the way she looks. "Although I always wanted to have a smooth, round face, I've discovered I'm fortunate in having hollow cheekbones. If you don't gain too much weight, your skin always stays pretty."

One more thing:

"It was lucky I always wore makeup because it protected my skin." Even though she was an outdoor girl, her skin was never overexposed to the sun. She always protected it with foundation makeup. And when she played tennis or went boating she always added a visored hat. As a result, her skin, after years in the sunshine, doesn't have that cracked parchment look too many outdoor women have.

"In staying young," she says, "a feeling of achievement and being loved makes a big difference—and having the ability to love. I think a lot of women aren't giving enough. I really like to give."

And give she still does—after all those years in show business. In fact, her vitality still astounds and amazes people who know her.

"You know," one reporter said recently, "there's got to be something *wrong* with that girl—she's just too good to be true. But I haven't yet found out what it is, and I've known her for nine years now."

Typical of her attitude is the kind of informal chatting she holds with her studio audience after each day's hour-and-a-half show is over.

"Please come by and see us again," she tells them. "You've been great. And listen, if you have any trouble getting tickets, mention my name. I've got pull around here."

That's great stuff with the fans.

"Isn't she adorable?" one little old lady says to a friend. "She always reminds me of my sister when she was a little girl."

And a teenager in blue jeans says, "Boy, she's really cool."

She has that ability that every great performer must have: the knack of being all things to all people. It is one of the key factors in her success. And she is quite aware of its value, and pleasantly objective about her manipulation of it.

"I'm a terrific politician, you know," she says. "A real vote-getter. I work hard at it and it pays off."

In fact, it is not only profitable and agreeable to Dinah, it is essential to her emotional well-being.

It is one of the reasons that her hour-and-a-half syndicated talk show is still running, when other competitors' shows have bitten the dust. Her guest list reads like a *Who's Who* of show business, the sports scene, the intellectual world—and almost every other field of endeavor.

For example, within the space of a few weeks recently, Dinah talked to such top show business personalities as Alan Alda, Lauren Bacall, Stockard Channing, Raymond Burr, Sean Connery, Angie Dickinson, Michael Douglas, Barbara Bel Geddes, Larry Hagman, Charlton Heston, Judd Hirsch, Bob Hope, Ron Howard, Jack Lemmon, Patrick Macnee, Ricardo Montalban, Harry Morgan, Anthony Quinn, McLean Stevenson, Robert Wagner, Dennis Weaver, Orson Welles, and Betty White.

Singers and performers within the same period included Glen Campbell, Carol Channing, Chubby Checker, Vic Damone, Eydie Gorme, Phil Harris,

Shirley Jones, Eartha Kitt, Steve Lawrence, Liberace, and Anthony Newley.

The comics she had on deck were Lucille Ball, Carol Burnett, George Burns, Chevy Chase, Dom DeLuise, and Rich Little.

Sports luminaries included heavyweight champion Muhammad Ali, golfer Julius Boros, quarterback Terry Bradshaw, weightlifter Franco Columbu, baseball star Reggie Jackson, stunt motorcyclist Dennis Madalone, exquarterback and sports commentator Don Meredith, ice-skater JoJo Starbuck, and quarterback Roger Staubach.

At the same time, she interviewed people with interesting professions like F. Lee Bailey, criminal defense lawyer; Dr. William Burton, an expert in unusual musical instruments; John Mack Carter, editor of *Good Housekeeping Magazine*; Jacques Cousteau, oceanographer, and deep-sea diver; Beth Halacy, solar cooking exponent; David Kolatch, connoisseur of cheeses; Marty Leshner, travel authority; and Alfred Parker, architect.

And she interviewed three mayors: Corinne Freeman, of St. Petersburg, Florida; Maurice Ferre, of Miami, Florida; and Leonard Haber, of Miami Beach, Florida.

In addition, she found time to pair off Brad Davis, the star of the movie *Midnight Express,* with Billy Hayes, the man upon whose experiences the motion picture was based; she chatted with Christopher Reeve, the star of the motion picture hit *Superman*; and she talked with Cheryl Ladd, one of "Charlie's Angels," Cheryl's mother, Dolores Stoppelmor, and Cheryl's stand-in on the series, Cis Rundle.

A list like that, chock-full of well-known personalities, the brightest in the country, for that matter, attests to the fact that both fans and guests find it extremely hard to pass up her show—and impossible to forget her.

Nor is it strange that the men in her life find it extremely hard to forget her, either.

When Barbara Walters interviewed the still-unmarried Burt Reynolds in a recent ABC television special, she said that Burt's split-up with Dinah Shore must have been "like breaking up with the American flag."

And Burt agreed. "I knew that when we decided to just be very, very good friends that I would be the heavy. If she'd cut me with a knife and hit me with a beer bottle and thrown me down the street and run over me with her car, the papers would have said, 'Burt Runs Out on Dinah.' "

Well, as the *New York Daily News* commented, "What else can a cad expect?"

But the key comment came later on in the interview. Barbara Walters asked Burt, who he'd like to be if he could come back in another life as a member of the opposite sex.

"I'll tell you who," Burt answered with that famous cat-that-ate-the-canary Reynolds grin, "Dinah Shore, that's who!"

Glittering lives of famous people!
Bestsellers from Berkley